Twentieth Century Merstham

Twentieth Century

Merstham

Millennium in Merstham

Published by Millennium in Merstham 1999.

An imprint of Beverley Books,
8 London Road South, Merstham, Surrey RH1 3DT.

Copyright © A. B. de M. Hunter 1999.

All rights reserved. According to the Copyright Designs and Patents Act 1988, the proprietor hereby asserts his moral right to be identified as the author of this work. Without limiting the rights under copyright reserved above, no part of this publication may be reproduced, stored in or introduced into a retrieval system, or transmitted, in any form, or by any means (electronic, photocopying, recording or otherwise) without the prior written permission of the copyright owner of this book.

ISBN 0–9535866–0–X

Set in 11/12pt Bembo by
Kalligraphic Design Ltd., Horley, Surrey.

Printed and bound by
Antony Rowe Ltd., Chippenham, Wiltshire.

Inside covers: Maps of Merstham in 1914 and 1985

Contents

Calendar of events	2
Introduction	5
Architects, builders and developers	6
City folk	15
Education providers	26
Entertainment, sport and social influences	30
Farmers and forces servicemen	43
Government members	54
Horticulturists	62
Landed gentry	64
Lawyers and criminals	70
Literary and artistic characters	74
Medical practitioners	78
Priests, rectors and vicars	82
Those in trade and transport	95
Postscript	103
Index	105

Calendar of events

1902	April: Merstham celebrated King Edward VII with meal and games for 1,000 adults and 600 children.
1903	Roads gradually surfaced in tarmac. Bicycle craze followed.
1904	S. Merstham Horticultural Soc. Founded.
1905	Merstham Tunnel Mystery.
1909	Merstham Boy Scouts started.
1911	George V's Coronation.
1914	First World War starts – servicemen were all volunteers, until conscription in 1917.
1918	Nov. 11th: War ended.
1919	Merstham Women's Institute formed. Redhill – Merstham bus route (21) started.
1920	Merstham pageant in grounds of Merstham House.
1921	British Legion founded.
1923	Southern Railway formed out of LBSCR, SECR & LSWR.
1926	May: General Strike.
1928	Cinemas started showing talking films.
1930	Economic depression.
1932	Electrification of railway line South from Stoats Nest, Coulsdon.
1933	Surrey Review Order splits Merstham between Reigate & Banstead District Councils.
1934	Gatton Hall gutted by fire.
1935	Silver Jubilee of George V.
1937	May: King George VI Coronation. Merstham recreation ground Fete. Gatton Firework display.
1938	Spanish orphans quartered in Deans House. Nylon stockings introduced.
1939	Second World War starts: Conscription, Anderson shelters and evacuations.
1940	Canadian Army quartered in and around Merstham.
1941	April: All Saints hit by landmine – 9 killed, several injured.
1944	"Doodlebug" flying bombs – 3 killed in Rockshaw Road.
1945	War ends. Peace celebrations. Rationing continues for years.
1947	The Big Freeze – Merstham under snow 24 January to 10 March.
1948	Railways, power and health nationalised. Olympic Games torch route includes Merstham carrier.

1950/1	The LCC estate built in Merstham.
1953	Elizabeth II's Coronation. Big boost in television rentals.
1956	May is driest month since 1896. Suez crisis.
1957	Rock and Roll, Teddy Boys – and Sputniks.
1958	Gatwick Airport opened.
1960	Transistor radios. The Merstham Society formally instituted.
1961	Tristan de Cunha volcano eruption – refugees in Pendell camp.
1963	Great Train Robbery and the Profumo affair.
1964	Beatles and Stones, Mods and Rockers. Merstham's Wates estate.
1965	Short skirts and long hair. LCC replaced by GLC.
1969	Men on the Moon.
1970	Canada Hall Women's Institute founded.
1971	February 15: Decimal coinage introduced.
1973	VAT introduced. Britain joins EEC. MADS win through to Drama Festival finals.
1974	Reigate and Banstead boroughs merged.
1975/6	M23 and M25 motorways opened locally.
1977	Silver Jubilee – festivities by The Epiphany, Village hall exhibition. Candlelight procession.
1979	Quality Street Fair revived by rector.
1980	Mercer's Park opened.
1982	Falklands conflict. Gramophone records gave way to compact discs
1984	Gatwick Express introduced; reduction in commuter trains stopping at Merstham.
1986	GLC abolished. Reigate and Banstead assume responsibility for the estate.
1987	October 15/16: Hurricane sweeps across S.E. England leaving massive devastation.
1989	Berlin wall dismantled. End of the Cold War.
1992	Economic recession.
1994	Channel Tunnel opened.
1996	Railways privatised.
1998	Merstham Millennium committee set-up.

Sand and brick works, Nutfield Road, in the 1930s

Introduction

With the millennium, Merstham celebrates at least thirteen centuries of existence, as we know from a document in the British Museum, which records its existence as a Saxon parish in 675 AD. Others have charted the ebb and flow of its fortunes in the intervening years[1], but it is our intention to commemorate the recent century: not so much the fabric of this ever changing dormitory village, but rather the people that contributed to its character over this period.

In selecting those who have touched the communal memory[2], one cannot pretend to have achieved a comprehensive catalogue of characters. These recent generations are more or less typical of other Surrey commuter belt villages, and may be considered as such for academic purposes. But for those of us in touch with their legacy, it is a more personal reminder of our community, and why it is so different from its neighbouring conurbations. Merstham evokes mixed reactions from its Reigate, Redhill and Nutfield neighbours, and is not as easily categorised. It is a varied community divided into three parishes: the "Old Merstham" of St. Katharine's, the "South Merstham" of All Saints, and the "Estate" of The Epiphany. But together, it is still MERSTHAM, despite attempts by the Post Office to make it part of Redhill, and the people mentioned here would not have dreamed of being considered to be from anywhere else.

Any number of people has contributed to this record, and we are delighted with the interest shown. It is, of course, invidious to single out individual contributors, but the committee is acutely aware of the time and effort provided by, and grateful to, Mary Bassett, Rosemary Stephens, Joyce Crosfield, Carole Goldsbrough, Jim Oliver, Percy Brown, John Callow, Norman Worsfold and the late Jim Charman. In addition, it would like to pay tribute to the legacy of Mrs. Gwynne (née Dawes) whose scrap book on her Merstham contemporaries is both a tribute to and example of how much these generations raised in Merstham still value this community long after they have left it for other counties or countries.

The Merstham Millennium Committee. *1999*

---

[1] Such as Rev. Woodhouse's *A brief guide to Merstham Parish* (1905), *The Story of Ancient Merstham* by Alfred Passmore (1912 – he was at Withyshaw on Rockshaw Road in the '30s), Llewellyn Williams' *Merstham Church: Its Builders & Parishioners* (1929), Mary Morris's *History of Merstham* (1971) and Alex Hunter's *Gentlemen of Merstham & Gatton 1519 -1979* (1993).

[2] The criteria was those who spent some time in Merstham in this century, but who also have ceased from active local activity at the time of writing. It includes some who made more of a mark elsewhere than locally, and some whose activities were entirely parochial. It is not expected to be exhaustive, but should at least be representative.

Architects, builders and developers

As most of Merstham was, for a long time, the personal estate of the Jolliffe family (Lord Hylton), there was little major development until the 1890s[3] and, even then, not of his volition: It had been Lord Monson, the then owner of the Gatton estate and Battlebridge Farm, who had sold land to the railways to create Merstham's first station in 1841, and his mother, the Countess of Warwick, who had developed "Warwick Town" South of Linkfield Lane as the future Redhill. A generation later, the seventh baron Monson put his Gatton estate up for auction in 1888, the Colman family topping a rival bid from a development syndicate. So it was Jeremiah Colman who sold the Battlebridge part of his new estate that was the other, leeward, side of the railway in 1891 to a Redhill draper, Robert **Nicol** to form the Albury & Dean's Road Building Association, the first of many such associations that created South Merstham. Mr. Nicol had his own house, Dean Lodge, built on the corner of Nutfield Road (no. 95) and the new Dean's Road. He set up communal tennis courts and a bowling green on what is now Melton Road, and was one of the principal donors to the new All Saints church that was built in 1898. He was also one of the founders of the Merstham Horticultural Society (at that time the full name was The South Merstham Horticultural and Cottage Garden Society) being its president from 1904 until his death in 1930. He had built a big department store in the centre of Redhill, which went up in a spectacular blaze in May 1901, but was rebuilt and remained the basis of his fortunes for decades thereafter. In many ways, Mr. Nicol can be considered the "father" of South Merstham. He was a "small, dapper, man" of firm liberal opinions, being of humble, Lincolnshire origins himself. He may have respected the conventions of the time, for example sending fellow tradesmen round to the tradesmen's door of his house, and referring to his houseboy always as "George" (though he actually was Bill Perkins, and then Percy Brown), but he was a caring parish council member and is on record, among other things, for trying to establish a recreational plot to literally get the children off the streets. In this he was frustrated, and it was

---

[3] Apart from the farms, there were only 8 private residences noted by Kelly's in 1887: Lord Hylton's Merstham House, the Rectory next door, The Grange, Hawthornden, Netherne House, Harps Oak, Coppice Lea & Oakley.

left to the Stephens to provide this gift a decade later. Whether Mr. Nicol's later sale of the tennis club land to Jack Deverill of Melton Road was indeed more for altruistic motives than personal gain (he is said to have disliked the way in which the club became elitist) may be questioned by a more cynical generation, but there can be no doubt that, without Mr. Nicol, South Merstham would never have been established as the community it became. The business, if not the house, was inherited by John Nicol who moved it to Station Road, Redhill, and then by his son, Don, who moved it again to what is now Geoff Taylors in Reigate High Street. As for Dean Lodge, Merstham, the County purchased it for a children's home[4] and later lodged a number of orphans from the Spanish Civil War there. Part of modern Chalkmead, a home for the elderly, now occupies the site.

With the death of the 2nd Lord Hylton in 1899, his son, the 3rd baron, who lived at their Radstock estate, started selective development in the rest of Merstham. In South Merstham (Nicol's tennis pavilion, to be exact), the Jolliffe agent, Harrie Stacey, held a sale of Albury Farm plots in 1901. To the North, the cart track through the Home Farm fields was developed as Rockshaw Road (being commented on by Hilaire Belloc on his walk to rediscover the old Pilgrims Way in 1902), the track up Merstham Hill became Church Hill and plots on existing roads were put on the market. There was a clear intent to ensure buildings in the old part of Merstham were to a high quality (contractually they had to be worth more than £600–£1,000 at sale!) and most of this period seem to be to the design of Paxton **Watson**. Paxton Watson came from the other end of Surrey, where he had been commissioned by Whitaker Wright to design Witley Park, a neo-Tudor mansion (similar to his contemporary, Sir Edwin Lutyens). It no longer exists, though Paxton Watson's Farnham buildings do survive. Paxton Watson's work in Merstham includes the Primary School (1898), Oakhurst in Nutfield Road and Rookwood in London Road South (1902) and a number of houses along Rockshaw Road and Church Hill (1903-5), many of which are thus included in Merstham's conservation area. He himself converted and lived in Barn House in Quality Street and later built Court Cottage next door for his sister, Georgina, a founder/member of the Merstham Women's Institute.

[4] Run by two true ladies, Miss Worsdell and Miss Hanratty, who would, for example, stretch their allowance to the limit to ensure each child had some "new" (ex-Jumble sale) clothes for their birthday party.

Lord Hylton already had a local builder. His "overseer" from the 1880s was Richard **Whitaker** who lived at Wisteria Cottage in the part of the High Street now known as Quality Street, with a builders yard that extended down the back. It is interesting to note that Whitaker was listed as "builder, decorator, contractor and plumber by appointment to the East Surrey Water Company" which had been formed to handle both the water supply needs of such new towns as Redhill and also to cater for the growing transition to indoor plumbing generally. His firm took corporate status, as R. Whitaker Ltd., and was the initial beneficiary of Paxton Watson's commissions (the firm's founder died in 1920, aged 74).

Building work was obviously halted during the First World War and the scarcity of materials immediately afterwards meant the trade had to make do with a different mix of materials, for example less timber and of a less seasoned, more softwood nature. Brook Road was developed along the edge of the stream bed by the Merstham Housing Society to offer homes to returning servicemen. Otherwise, it was the demand of outsiders for housing away from the smog-ridden City which encouraged the ribbon development of the 1920s and 30s. Merstham was typical of those Surrey railway villages that saw a big influx of professionals and artisans. The more expensive housing of "Old" Merstham, centred on the High Street, to the North and West of the railway, attracted more higher earning commuters than the no less recent, but somewhat cheaper, buildings in South Merstham, centred around Nutfield Road, to the leeward side of the steam-driven railways. It was an unfortunate division that mirrored the sharper divides of society at the time, similar to the perceived difference between Reigate and Redhill. For the local traders and builders, though, business was business in whichever parish it was located.

It was Mr. Whitaker who took on young Sidney **Francis**, one of the six children of David and Sarah Francis, David being coachman to Sir Jeremiah Colman of Gatton. Sidney learned the builder's trade quickly and efficiently, being something of a perfectionist, and eventually started his own business, opening his Yard on a piece of land in Albury Road given to him by his father-in-law, Mr. Stribbling. Peter Stephens of Coppice Lea took an interest in the South Merstham developments, both in terms of helping set up one-off mortgage associations, and in recommending builders of proven worth, so it is not surprising to find S. J. Francis got an ever increasing number of jobs where quality was required. The inter-war years still demanded the sort of attention to detail that one associates with their Victorian parents and the three local firms, Whitakers, S. J. Francis & Son and Pink & Oram worked well together in friendly rivalry on buildings all over, and beyond, the Merstham area. Bill Perkins had started building in South Merstham in the 1920s but never expanded beyond that group of roads. What was more acceptable then than it would be today was that both S. J. Francis and J. J. Pink were parish councillors. Sydney Francis' eldest son, Jim, joined the firm in 1932 and earned his inheritance: At its height the firm employed 80 men. Not long after Whitakers closed in the late '60s, Jim Francis sold his business to Mansells of Croydon. Jim also took a deep interest in Merstham's Youth Centre, the Boys Brigade and the Merstham Horticultural Society, his well laid-out garden at 23 High Street being a good example of the typical high standard one has long been used to in this part of England. He died in 1987, much mourned because of the keen interest he took in keeping the village vibrant and attractive. It is through him and his widow, Pauline Francis, that their son-in-law, David Battie, well known to followers of *The Antiques Roadshow*, gave four different talks to The Merstham Society on the art market.

Mr. J. J. **Pink** was another early arrival in the South Merstham parish, advertising his construction skills in the 1909 Horticultural Show brochure. He was soon closely involved with the community, being elected to the Parish Council in 1918, an active member of the Cricket Club and founder of the Merstham Quoit Club at the Railway Arms. His son, S. Thomas Pink, joined up with Wilfred **Oram** to form Pink & Oram, based in Endsleigh Road, and bought a stretch of Battlebridge farm land for development. The consequent Orpin Road, developed in 1931, derives from their combined names. Thomas Pink was elected councillor in 1935 and served in the Second World War, being awarded an MC. On his return, he was duly elected Chairman of the Merstham British Legion. He lived in 181 Nutfield Road, with his partner Wifred Oram on one side in 179, and "young" Charlie H. Pink (so as not to be confused with "old" Charlie Pink, his uncle, both of whom were active players for Merstham Cricket Club) on the other side, in 183. Included among the many members of the Pink family listed on their suitably pink coloured marble tombstone in St. Katharine's churchyard is 31 year old Charles Pink who died of his wounds in 1944. In the late '70s, Pink & Oram became a short-lived double glazing business in the High Street, but there were no Pinks or Orams in the business by then.

The next World War again interrupted further development, though the Green Belt restrictions, enacted in 1938, would have acted as a constraint in any event. The numerous committees, voluntary groups and, of course, the Home Guard acted as a unifying force for the two Merstham communities in the early '40s and the village emerged as a more focused and coherent settlement from the dark days of deprivation, bombing and disruption. It was thus viewed as most unfortunate when the open land either side of Bletchingley Road was developed by the London County Council as one of its satellite estates for the homeless from the battle-scarred city. Lord Hylton had planned to sell off this part of his Merstham estate before the War, with the usual quality covenants that are attached to earlier Jolliffe land sales, but had been checked by the Green Belt. The War created a reinterpretation of the purpose of that legislation, so that the new Government had no difficulty in giving consent, on appeal, to planning permission in 1949. By 1952, 1,560 houses had been built to LCC designs, and on the erroneous assumption of limited car ownership. The houses on Bletchingley Road, Radstock Way and Bolsover Grove were designated for the higher income (or "white collar" as it was then termed) families. Because the estate was between the Peters quarries to the North and the Laporte/BIS excavations to the South, many of the road names were chosen to represent other English quarries (e.g.: Purbeck, Portland, Mansfield, Delabole, while "malm stone" is another name for the "greensands" extracted from Nutfield). The lessons of South Merstham went unheeded: the estate was a separate parish, had its own shopping street, schools and, of course, was run by a different County authority. More important, the new residents were virtually all Londoners of the same generation and state (to have arrived at the top of the housing lists at the same time), compared with the mixed generations that had developed over time in the established Merstham parishes. For sure, it developed its own community spirit (fostered by the annual Carnival, the clubs and schools) but it never really connected with "top Merstham". Only now, 40 years on, with a wider demographic profile, greater home ownership and the absorption of the estate into the borough's responsibility, can one look forward to a more integrated Merstham.

There have been a number of architects (as well as consulting engineers, estate agents and others involved with property) living in the village, but Tim **Alleyn** was the only one who was also a councillor, becoming mayor in the late '60s. As a result he became an ex-officio magistrate and served on the bench for about a decade. Lt. Col. Alleyn, as he then was, arrived in Merstham during the War, moving into the Old Tye Place, by the entrance to the Primary School. Released from service, as he put it, in 1946, he reverted to his trade as a chartered architect. At this point he was 38 and, like his predecessor in the house, Chris Jarchow, very much a gregarious member of the community. One of his best remembered parts in MADS was as Shakespeare in Shaw's *Dark Lady of the Sonnets*. He was a borough councillor from 1955, being mayor for 1966-8. In the mid '50s he moved next door to The Saddlery which had been a harness-makers. When Sir Dick White left the area in '59, he bought Wisteria Cottage in Quality Street and later moved to The Bell House, all his homes being in a narrow orbit of the High Street. His contribution to the borough was his involvement in 1965/66 in establishing Centenary House in Redhill, a day centre for the elderly. His legacy to Merstham, however, is the two churches on the estate, The Epiphany and St. Teresa's. He himself was a Catholic and a Knight of the Holy Sepulchre, a sort of senior echelon of Catholic laity. When he was 60 he qualified as an Arbitrator, and rose to become chairman of the Arbitration Council. He died in 1983, aged 75; his second wife, Margaret, lives in Reigate.

The growth of Merstham has so far been restricted to occasional infilling so that it still has a lower density of housing than the commuter area to its North in the Greater London Area. With the rapid increase in property values, it has been difficult to resist putting every spare patch of land to use. By themselves the Green Belt restrictions provide little protection; it is the willingness of the borough and county councils to defend the local infrastructure and services from the pressures of massive increases in homes and offices that makes the difference. Through the efforts of such people as councillor Ernie Crowe, Redhill has become the local shopping and office hub, leaving Merstham to be one of its residential satellites. The village has also benefited from the landscaping of one of the nearby BIS pits to form Mercers Lake recreational centre, and from the transformation of some of Colebrooke's fields into Reigate Hill golf club which saved the public footpath to Gatton from being ploughed over annually. The main architect of Mercers Lake was Laporte Industries' resettlement officer, Ron **Mountford**, a keen horticulturist and local historian. He was also the first chairman of the Chalkmead League of Friends from 1972 (organising the South Merstham Wheelchair Push), and it was in keeping with his keen interest in the community that his sudden demise should have been while taking another party to the Keukenhof tulip gardens at Easter time, 1983.

The longest lasting amenity in Merstham is its section of the former Pilgrim's Way, the origins of which go back centuries before Thomas à Becket's shrine became an object of pilgrimage. The route was popularised by Hilaire Belloc's book in 1903, when he had to make a detour round Merstham House, and again by the Shell guides of the 1930s, at which time Tolsworth Manor, up by Alderstead Heath, was acquired by the Youth Hostel Association. The route became further obscured by post-war development, so that the Countryside Commission proposed the nearest rights of way be designated "The North Downs Way" in 1963. One can appreciate the amount of negotiation required, since it took another 15 years before it could be officially opened in its entirety, since when it has been walked by hundreds of thousands of ramblers. Of the many local walkers, Iain **Ogilvie** stands out. A civil engineer by profession, he returned from managing the Bombay Docks enlargement to a Head Office job and a daily commute from 38 London Road South. His hobby had always been mountaineering and he had been awarded the MBE for a courageous attempt to save a friend who had fallen down a sheer snow face on An Teallach. A stroke put a stop to serious mountaineering but he carried on walking the Scottish and Lakeland Hills for years afterwards. He completed all the Munros[5] by the time he was 70 ("I'm still fit for twenty-four miles a day"), in 1983. He and his wife, Bernardine, kept the Scottish traditions and it was fitting that it was The Royal Scottish Museum that accepted his gift shortly before his death in 1997 of 20 scale model boats that he had made himself.

The main, and most dramatic, change to the area this century has been the building of the motorways in the late 1970s. Merstham was the first to experience the development of the M23 and M25 and fought hard to have them re-routed, with a committee chaired by Brian Webbe. To no avail: The M25

---

[5] Some 277 Scottish peaks over 3,000 ft. as listed by Dr. Munro in the Nineteenth Century.

The newly rebuilt station in 1907

Merstham's volunteer fire brigade by the gates to Merstham House

motorway was cut straight through the parish, making a mockery of this coomb's official designation as "The Surrey Hills Area of Outstanding Natural Beauty". As a sweetener, the County created an official "Conservation Area" either side of the motorway. The ancient Merstham marsh exacted some tribute: At least one massive earthmoving vehicle sank so far down that it was duly left to form part of the foundations rather than be retrieved. The M23 was opened in 1974 and this section of the M25 (built by W. French & Co.) a couple of years later, but its use only really took off once the circuit was completed with the opening of the Leatherhead section in October 1985. The M25 was widened to eight lanes by Laing's in 1997/8, which resulted in an increase in height of the mound on the Northern edge of the estate. A Merstham resident is now about 15 minutes away from Gatwick airport, an hour away from the Channel tunnel, and in relatively easy reach of the rest of England, a big improvement on the previous situation.

City folk

As a commuter station based neatly in a fold of the Surrey Hills, considered to be a beauty spot until the motorways came, Merstham attracted a number of senior men from the City's trades and professions. Colin Stradling remembers as a boy seeing the early-morning procession of men in suits, bowler hats and umbrellas going to the station, passing en route their gardeners going in the opposite direction. In the early days of the steam LBSC trains, the "City commuters of Reigate, Bletchingley and Merstham seemed to own it – it was not unknown for it to wait for latecomers"[6]. The City of London's main businesses were Shipping, Insurance and Banking in this period (in this order of wealth creation pre-war, reverse order post-war) and Merstham became the home for representatives of all three:

Of the shipping fraternity, William **Grieve** built Ringwood at Gatton Point, at that time within Merstham parish, in the 1890s. He was originally from Scotland but had built up a strong City-based trading operation with Burma, mainly in rice. He had five children, only one of whom was destined to live beyond 35 years old. One daughter, Margaret, died in 1901 and it was in her memory that the Grieves gave St. Katharine's its 6th bell. The boys all volunteered for service in the First World War: The youngest had only just got married at the time and was killed at Ypres in 1915 before his own son was born. The eldest, Maj. James Grieve, joined up as an ordinary trooper in King Edward's Horse, earning a commission into the RHA in 1915. Promotion followed rapidly, though he was wounded (and earned his MC) in the Somme in 1916. He lasted until the spring of 1918 when he too was killed. The one in between, Charles, went through the war safely with the Gordon Highlanders, only to be murdered in Ireland during the rebellion there in 1920. His body was never found. William Grieve had played an active part in both Merstham parishes but, without his sons, moved to Putney where he died in 1927. Ringwood had been sold to a Mr. Smart who renamed it The Hawthorns. The surviving daughter was buried in St. Katharine's relatively recently. Despite the tribulations of this

---

[6] As remembered by Norman Worsfold, who ran the station bookstall. Certainly the author recalls how, even in the delays and cancellations of the '80s, he was occasionally able to prevail upon the driver at East Croydon to make an unscheduled stop at Merstham.

generation, William Grieve's grandson ended up an eminent QC and MP for Solihull 1964-83.

When George Jolliffe inherited the Hylton title and estates from his father, the second baron, he was already living on the Radstock estates and had less interest in Merstham House, the family seat[7]. Accordingly he let Merstham House to Andrew **Walker**, who was the elderly Managing Director of Bovril Ltd. Bovril had been invented by his colleague, Mr. John Lawson Johnson, in 1887 and had become so popular that the word was used in the 1930s as slang for a brothel! This is no reflection on Andrew Walker, though. Some of his descendants still live in Reigate and have a splendid photograph of this heavily bearded Victorian gentleman surrounded by his huge family outside Merstham House. He retired in 1913, aged 75, and died a couple of years later. His wife was the better known of the couple locally, hosting the Merstham pageant in the grounds of Merstham House. She died in 1928 and Lord Hylton tried first to let the property and then to develop it. The next occupiers were the senior staff officers of the Canadian division quartered in the area for most of the War. Of the many Walker children, his third son was Maj. Hector Walker MC who married late in life – and after a great deal of encouragement – Polly, sister of John Topham Richardson of Harps Oak. They lived at Woodfield Place on Harps Oak Lane, and were well remembered for their support of the Merstham & District Operatic Society, Hector being particularly good in Gilbert & Sullivan roles.

Of Andrew Walker's daughters, the eldest, Helen, married H. Leonard **Puckle,** a City chartered accountant. After Helen's death in 1941, Leonard married Grace, widow of William Nicholson, and moved into her house on Church Hill. After his death in 1948, Grace moved next door into Woodlands House and lived there until her own death in 1961. History has it that she left the family wine stocks in Church Hill House (Woodlands House having no cellar), sending her gardener next door with a wheelbarrow to collect a bottle or two as and when needed! It was Grace, the second Mrs. Puckle, who donated the garden site above the Churchyard to St Katharine's.

Of those involved in Insurance, the earliest resident was Peter **Stephens** of Thomas Stephens & Sons, insurance brokers, in the City (starting in EC4 but gradually moving nearer to Lloyds

---

[7] Merstham House used to lie between Gatton Bottom and the modern motorway. It was pulled down in the early 1950s when there was no demand for such buildings. See p.66.

in EC3). He had married Lottie (Charlotte) Simpson of Wray Park in 1902 and bought Rookwood on London Road South from a doctor. Lottie Stephens became a firm friend of Maud Roffey, from The Grange, these two extremely competent ladies taking an active interest in the pre-war suffragette movement. Together with another neighbour, Ulricha Jarchow, they founded the Merstham Nursing Association in those days before the National Health, recruiting Nurse Augarde as the local nurse, midwife and general medical officer. After the First World War, Lottie served on the War Pensions Committee, attending to the needs of those local families whose menfolk had gone, mostly voluntarily, to serve in that war (and there were few Merstham families not involved). As their four children approached their teens, the Stephens moved, in 1919, to Coppice Lea, the Pelly's former home, and took on the small estate that went with the property. With the growing concern about the distance of the only recreational area, Alderstead Heath, from the young of South Merstham, it was the Stephens who donated some 5 acres of their land to form the present Recreation Ground behind Albury Road. Lottie served on the Merstham parish council until 1933 when it was taken into the new Reigate Rural District Council. She was also a much respected member of the Primary School Board. She was only 56 at her death in 1937. Peter remarried and lived on through the next war, dying in 1951. It was his youngest child, Anthony, who took over Coppice Lea: Anthony had gone into the family insurance business, being briefly interrupted by the need to don uniform and see service overseas for the second World War. He married Rosemary Webbe in 1941 and, together, they became increasingly involved in local schools. Rosemary joined the board of Eothen School in 1955, becoming Chairman three years later. Both Stephens were also both very much involved in the foundation of Cobham Hall school. But it is in connection with the transition of owner-run schools to corporate charities that they are best remembered. In 1959 the headmistress/owner of Micklefield School in Reigate asked the Stephens to help plan a successor, and they set about getting a structure and new headmistress in place. When, in 1961, the School became a corporate entity, Rosemary Stephens became Chairman and presided over its period of growth in quality and numbers for the next twenty years. A similar need was met for Dunottar (1961), and again at the Hawthorns (1978), when Anthony used all his negotiating skills to fend off imminent bankruptcy and create a more secure basis for future governance. He retired from Lloyds in 1970 but not from village life: He is well remembered for his regular attendance at the bi-monthly auctions run in the Village Hall by Harold Williams & Bennett, the local estate agents, employing the same bargain hunting techniques which he had used on behalf of others since before the war. The couple still lives at The Glade House at the motorway end of Quality Street.

Most of the City folk who arrived in Merstham at the beginning of the century bought the then expensive houses in old Merstham. Albury Edge, the first of the new villas on Rockshaw Road in 1903, was for R. Percy **Sellon**, son of a sapper officer and nephew of John Sellon, the founder of British Electrical Engineering Co. He was 40 years old when he came to Merstham and was already director of several companies (Johnson Matthey & Co., the bullion dealers, Otis Elevators and some 25 different traction and electrical supply companies) so was not entirely in his uncle's shadow, though he did succeed him as Managing Director of Johnson Matthey & Co. He would have been one of hundreds of City commuters who moved to Merstham, but he also found time to be concerned with the village's amenities, taking an active role on the Parish Council. He was also a teetotaller and contributed to the foundation of the Merstham Village Club, when it was set up after the First World War, so that returning servicemen would have an alternative to the pub as a meeting place. When he died, in 1928, Sir Harry Renwick wrote that Percy was "well read, modest and had a strong sense of duty", attributes one rarely hears applied to captains of industry these days. His wife, Gwenyth, stayed on at Albury Edge until her death, aged 78, in 1945. She was a familiar figure in the Red Cross activities locally. They had a son who understandably did not try to match his father's business reputation.

Returning to the Walker family, another daughter, Rosamund, had married Henry **Nicholson** who was a Clerk to the Commissioners of the Inland Revenue for the City, one of a select band of senior tax lawyers, in simple terms. He was at Clavadel from at least 1909 from where he also ran the Merstham Rifle Club. It may surprise a later generation to be told that this Club used to use the Merstham School for indoor practice, being a sport that is now viewed as incompatible with current school mores. When Henry died, his widow moved to Meadowside in Quality Street, which her son, A. T. R. "Binks"

Nicholson inherited after the Second World War. He was a chartered accountant who went into the family firm of H. Leonard Puckle & Co., before going on to become Company Secretary of Watney Mann & Co. Binks is well remembered as Captain of Merstham Cricket Club. His wife, Anne, had spent most of the war doing decoding work in Bletchley Park.

To the North of the parish, John **Topham Richardson**, son of G. G. Richardson of Redhill, moved into Harps Oak, London Road North, in about 1910. He would have just retired at 60 from his family malt business (Timothy Richardson & Sons) on the Hop Exchange that operated in Southwark, primarily for the brewing industry. He had also followed in his father's footsteps as a JP and local borough councillor and, at Reigate's charter jubilee banquet in 1913, amused the gathering by quoting from his father's diary of borough needs in the 1860s. Certainly he was a generous benefactor to a number of causes. His wife, Katherine, was some 14 years younger and became an active member of the village's W.I. on its formation after the First World War. At this time part of the proceeds of the War Memorial Fund were allocated towards the construction of a Village Hall, though there had been a difference of opinion between those who wanted it to be primarily for the benefit of returning service men, and those who thought it should be put to wider use. The Village Hall involved a considerable sum of money, and the Topham Richardsons were among the most active in getting it designed and built (Pink & Oram started before all the money had been collected). So it is fitting that there should be a couple of memorial stones to two of their daughters incorporated in the foundations of the Village Hall. For the family was struck by the double loss of these two girls, both 19 at their deaths in 1924 and 1929 respectively. Katharine was widowed in 1933, but stayed on at Harps Oak. In about 1938, she also bought land released from use as allotments, on the other side of the railway from Wells Nurseries, for use by the Merstham Scouts, though the intervention of the next War meant she never saw the plan come to fruition; she died after an operation in London in 1945. Nevertheless, the scouts had their building a decade later, and one of those present at the opening was a surviving daughter of the Topham Richardsons, Elizabeth (Lady Gordon Cumming). The hall was used by the Merstham Horticultural Society for its 1977 Silver Jubilee Show, and annually thereafter.

Another family connected with Insurance and Shipping was

the Bowring family. The firm, C. T. Bowring & Co., had a solid reputation, particularly with regard to its Canadian interests, well before Cyril and Clary **Bowring** moved into The Georgian House on Rockshaw Road in 1925. Cyril had been an infantry officer in the first war and had just completed a stint in the family firm's New York office when he arrived in Merstham. At 39 he was a welcome addition to a village that had lost so many of his generation. In no time at all he had become Captain of the Merstham Cricket Club, a position he held throughout the Second World War, organising a game against the Canadians quartered in the area in return for a softball match. With the formation of the Home Guard, Cyril was appointed commander of the Merstham contingent, reporting to the Reigate area headquarters. As in the case of the later comedy program *Dads Army*, the natural meeting place would have been the Village Hall but, despite Cyril being chairman of the Village Club, the trustees would only tolerate that if they wore plimsolls (trainers) rather than their studded boots! Of their three children, Derrick had started off in the family business in Newfoundland, coming back to England in uniform. His Canadian bride-to-be made her own way to join him in England, turning up at The Georgian House in August 1940 dressed in only a pyjama top, trousers and oil-soaked raincoat, with a toothbrush and flannel in a paper bag. The cargo boat on which she had taken passage had been torpedoed en route and she was lucky both to escape the explosion that ripped apart her initially-allotted berth, and to be later picked up from her lifeboat by a destroyer. Even their wedding reception was interrupted by yet another air-raid warning. But *Amor vincit omnia*, as the saying goes. Derrick's sister, Sonia, was another Merstham lady who did war work in Bletchley Park and the younger son, Norman, was only 23 when he was reported "missing from air operations in December 1943" being shot down over Leipzig.

One of Norman Bowring's school friends had been Ronald **Prentice** who, early in the war, became an Intelligence Officer joining the SOE in Cairo and then, in 1943/4, in Macedonia in that messy melange of warring factions. He returned to marry Sonia Bowring in 1948, just months before her father was diagnosed with the cancer that was to kill him. The Prentices set up home at Standish on Rockshaw Road in 1953. The Lloyds

Merstham Cricket Ground

insurance market must have seemed dull compared with his formative years. Still, Ron took on his father-in-law's mantle as Captain of the Merstham Cricket Club and kept it the social focal point of the village, before television changed our recreational priorities. The intention to link an orbital motorway to an M23 at Merstham was first announced in 1967 and Ron Prentice joined forces with Brian Webbe in setting up the Merstham Protection Society, with Brian as chairman, to try to have the motorways sited away from the village. It was through no lack of effort that it failed, having raised substantial sums to make appropriate legal representation. From the government's point of view, the affected population was small and the constituency unalterably secure for the then opposition party. With the advent of the motorways began the exodus of some of the wealthier City types, particularly those at the Eastern end of Rockshaw Road, which was dissected by the M23. Some remained and continued to contribute to Merstham's community generally, and St. Katharine's especially. Ron Prentice was one such; he was 65 at his death in 1984. Another ex-serviceman involved in the Insurance business, John **Lee,** first came to newly-built Field End in Harps Oak Lane with his family, from which he joined the other commuters walking to catch one of the then frequent trains to London Bridge. He later moved to Alderstead Farm and then Quality Street. He shared with Tim Alleyn and Michael Callow an interest in sailing, though it was Michael Callow of Relf House on Rockshaw Road, an engineer by trade, who built his own boat and sailed it all over the world. John Lee's leadership ability was well demonstrated as chairman of the Merstham Society, a position he held from 1987 to 1998, when he became its president.

Col. "Jock" **Hunter** MBE bought Clavadel in Rockshaw Road (from Mrs. Nicholson) after the Second World War. He was a director of Messel & Co, the stockbrokers, at a time when this profession epitomised easy money and the Surrey commuting area was referred to as the "gin and jag. belt". He would have been a cut above the average, though, as he became deputy chairman of the Stock Exchange, about the time that he moved further down the road to Tanglewood, swapping houses with the widow of Merstham's other stockbroker, Arthur Moy, when her son went to Reigate. Jock Hunter was another strong supporter of St. Katharine's, the Horticultural Society, and other community efforts, especially the Merstham Peace

Commemoration Committee which he chaired. They had two sons and two daughters, the latter both being widowed young. Grace was an active supporter of the Friends of the Elderly. Once Jock retired, they moved to West Sussex, not far from the Bensons.

Henry **Benson**, or Lord Benson as he has since become, was another eminent City character. He started life in South Africa and, as one would expect of the grandson of Francis Cooper of the accountants' firm, Cooper Brothers, became a chartered accountant, being appointed a partner of the family business at 25 years old, in 1934. In the next 30 years he took the firm to a pre-eminent position among the top six City accountants. As senior partner, he was knighted in 1964, and was also president of the English Institute of Chartered Accountants in 1966. It was at this time that he came to Merstham with his family, buying The Red House on Rockshaw Road. His public advisory roles at this time included the National Trust, the Horse Racing Industry and the much changed *The Times*. He was awarded his GBE in 1971 and became advisor to Harold Wilson's Government from 1975, at the same time becoming Treasurer of the newly created Open University. He was elevated to the Peerage in that government's outgoing honours list in 1980, but declined to follow the Labour whip, preferring the individuality of the cross benches. By then he had already moved to Sussex. His wife was better known locally, being active in St. Katharine's affairs and a regular visitor to the local elderly.

Another post-war family to arrive on Rockshaw Road, at The Mere, were the Lachelins: Pierre **Lachelin**, as his name suggests, was the son of a Frenchman, but very English in every aspect. He was a director of a merchant bank, Philip Hill Higginson Erlangers Ltd., unusual in that its origins were in the West End, rather than the City. Merchant banks were supposed to live more off their wits than their assets, but one needed a big balance sheet to compete in a global market, so members of the Accepting House Committee were forced to merge to survive, Pierre Lachelin's bank being put together with M. Samuel & Co. by Sir Kenneth Keith in 1965 to form Hill Samuel. It was a rewarding time to be a merchant banker and some of Pierre Lachelin's activities can be guessed from his other directorships: He was chairman of Meredith & Drew, the biscuit makers, vice chairman of Hedges & Butler, wine merchants, and on the boards of British Land, Metal Closures, and the General & Commercial Investment Trust Ltd. He was equally active locally. He was on St. Katharine's church council and, together with Jock Hunter and the Treasurer, Roger Constant[8], established the Stipend Augmentation Fund, so as to add some income to the pay of the Rectors. He was also financial advisor to the bishop of Southwark. His first wife, Joan, was an active supporter of the W.I. being its secretary in 1952 and president from the following year to 1956. In 1964 a legacy left by Mrs. Lachelin allowed the bells of St. Katharine's to be re-hung, with the addition of two extra ones (one provided by Mr. Lachelin, the other by Mr. Constant) making a peal of 8 in all. Pierre Lachelin died in 1977 aged just 77.

On Rockshaw Road, Alan and Mary **Fogg** have provided impressive support to community groups and to individuals. Alan Fogg was a director of PA International, one of the leading firms of business consultants, and gave excellent professional advice to many including St. Katharine's parochial council, and especially to the Royal Philanthropic Society at a critical time in its long history. It had been operating a reformatory farm school in Redhill since 1849, the exact nature of which changed with each change in applicable legislation. In 1973 it had to move from being a sort of educational remand centre to being more part of the Government's community care programme, losing control of the administration of its school to Wandsworth council. This put the Royal Philanthropic Society in an awkward organisational and financial situation that called for expert advice. Alan Fogg was on hand and became its chairman in 1982. It took some years to sort out the legal possibilities and negotiate with all parties involved but, by 1986, the society was in a position to serve notice that it would no longer be providing its premises from 1988, and the School duly closed[9] and the property was sold. The Society then relocated to Westerham, Kent, and continues to fulfil its original purpose as a charitable foundation for the benefit of young offenders, but on a broader basis and mainly in the Southern Home Counties. Having achieved this restructuring, Alan retired as chairman, with a well-earned MBE, in 1990, though he remains on its general committee, as does another Merstham resident, Joyce Crosfield.

There were, and are, of course, many other characters who

---

[8] Roger Constant was partner of a City Solicitors firm and lived first at Woodfield Place on Harps Oak Lane, then Cucksmead on Church Hill.
[9] Alan Moore of 25 The Crossways compiled a summary of the RPS records, which is available in Redhill Library.

have made their mark in London, some, doubtless, of greater seniority than those mentioned above. Merstham's popularity as a residence was, after all, based on its being one of the nearest patches of Green Belt with close communications to the metropolis. Those who have been highlighted above are those who have been more noticeable to the local community, those who have supported local activities and have touched upon the minds and hearts of their fellow residents. In any event, the village residents are now less reliant on the City. This is partly due to the 1992 recession which particularly affected City jobs (and required extra dole staff to be seconded from London to help out at Redhill's hard pressed Unemployment Centre) and partly due to the motorways that in effect have created a new, East/West employment catchment area along the M25 corridor. Twentieth Century Merstham was largely determined by its railway links to London; in the next millennium, it will be quite differently oriented.

Education providers

The Old School House in Quality Street had been the village school providing basic education for children up to 10, later 11, years old (the legal limit) since 1849. With the sudden increase in families moving into South Merstham, a new building was commissioned by the local School Board, and duly built, in 1898, at the top of Bletchingley Road (this bit being re-named School Hill), opening for business in 1899. Thus the village's School has already celebrated a century[10] of service to the community. The 1902 Education Act made Merstham School the responsibility of Surrey County, and the two senior positions were re-staffed, Charles Ball being appointed head of the Boys' section and Miss Alice Aldridge head of the Girls' section. Mrs. Harriet Priddy continued to run the Infants, Department, which she had done in the old school since 1896. The three of them set the foundations of what was a disciplined, yet caring, training ground. They retired in 1911, 1909 and 1914 respectively. The new team was led by 33 year old Charlie **Wall** who was to spend his next 33 years in that role. Despite the distractions of two World Wars, the increase in school leaving age to 14 in 1918, and the steady increase in families moving into the area in this period, he set and achieved a high standard in the classrooms, on the sports field and in the swimming pool. For virtually all the children that passed through this school, it was their sole formal education, and it is clear from a number of sources that Mr. Wall held their respect and affection. He used to ferry team members to matches in his open-topped Humber, for which the senior boys made a timber garage under the direction of the woodwork master, Mr. Hoffer. Mr. Wall lived in the School House at the London Road South entrance to the school with his wife, Lily, who also taught at the school, initially part-time. However, following the tragic loss of their own daughter in the post war 'flu epidemic, she worked full-time from 1920 to 1935 when she retired through ill health. Charlie Wall retired in 1944, just before the school was temporarily closed due to the spate of flying bombs that summer. One landed on the Council depot by the nearby railway bridge, killing instantly both a woman in the adjoining cottage and a driver sitting in the cab of his lorry. It severely damaged the

---

[10] The occasion was marked by John Neil's *Memories of One Hundred Years* (1989) which sets out a record of the School and its origins.

British Legion building on one side, and shattered windows of the school on the other. Some of the school ceilings also fell but, luckily, apart from a few cuts, there were no injuries among the children or staff. Schooling was suspended for a few months. The Walls retired to the Old Manor house in Quality Street bought for them by the Stephens, though Lily died only a few months later. The Butler Education Act of that same year meant it would thereafter be just a primary school, its children moving on at 11 years old. Of the other teachers of this period, Henry Nightingale (or "Punch" as one generation of children called him) served the longest, and had been on the staff for 39 years when the 1944 Act gave him the right to call himself "qualified" for salary scale purposes!

Another school, the Hawthorns, was also originally in Merstham's parish. In 1926 the Bull family purchased The Hawthorns at Gatton Point for their son, Dudley **Bull,** to operate as a private boys' school. He was joined shortly by his brother, Chris, and their sister Margaret, as matron, and their respective wives, Muriel and Ruth, also became part of the management team. In 1927 there were just 22 boys at the school, barely enough to field two sides of football or cricket, and it remained small, struggling through the Depression, until 1939. At that time, with the start of the Second World War, most other private schools closed or moved to safer parts of the country but the Bulls decided, with the agreement of the parents, to stay put (the Grieves had built the house with good solid cellars) and it paid off in terms of an increase of numbers from then on, a tribute also to the Bulls' cultivation of both an all-round education and a genial family atmosphere. The Bulls set quite an example: Dudley was for a time the Scout District Commissioner, and was also well known for his support of the local dramatic society ("MADS"), while Chris was as deeply involved with the cricket club (the MCC, of course). Dudley was also a co-founder of the Merstham Society, being its chairman from 1975 to 1983.

The main founder of the Merstham Society, though, was Miss Cecile **Hummel**, or "Hummy" as she was known to her friends. She had originally started a small school in Chipstead, moving to Merstham to open The Grange School when the Roffey's former home came on the market before the Second World War. She evacuated her school to the West Country at the outbreak of hostilities, only to find her house commandeered by the Army on her return in the quiet period of early 1940. So she moved, appropriately enough, to The Old School House in Quality Street until she could re-occupy The Grange after the War. It was a prep. school for girls, taking pre-prep. boys as well, with the three Miss Battiscombes providing a stalwart nucleus to the staff. In the mid '50s she changed the school to a nursery school for children from 4 to 8 years old and moved from The Grange into a specially constructed smaller building that has since been converted into the bungalows of Grange Court. She had quite a personality and, apart from a dedicated approach to education, is also remembered as the instigator of the pageants staged in Reigate Priory. She retired from teaching in 1959, and Miss Hope Mason took over the school. Miss Hummel's involvement with the Merstham Society arose out of a Lenten study group in 1957. Encouraged by the then rector, Mr. Poole, she held evening meetings of "The St. Katharine's Parents Guild" in The Grange and The Golden Wheel to discuss problems associated with bringing up young children locally. The initial interest waned but the surviving committee members in 1960 resolved to set up a broader-based society to promote friendship and social contact in the village, the meeting place from 1962 to 1988 being the new hall of Merstham Primary School. Miss Hummel stayed on, as vice president, while Jim Danckwerts ran it, until she was recruited as an expert on historical costumes, to set up and run a historical costume museum in Castle Howard, North Yorkshire in 1964. "She was a larger-than-life character, very warm-hearted, and loved drama; life was never dull with her"[11].

The Hawthorns School had the same problems as had Merstham's Primary School, with scarcity of space inside and traffic hazards outside. So the Bulls decided to move to the Hawthorns' present location, at Pendell Court near Bletchingley, in 1961. Dudley and Muriel Bull retired to The Grange some 8 years later, his position as Headmaster falling on an Old Boy, Geoffrey Learner, whose family came from Redhill. It was during this period that the School experienced its first real threat: In 1978 the Reigate Grammar School became part of the private sector, and a direct competitor to The Hawthorns. The Board, with some advice from Anthony Stephens, made the necessary changes, and the head was able to ensure continuity of educational standards. Dudley was millennium born, dying in 1996 aged 96.

[11] The tribute is by Gillian Penny, née Bull, Hawthorns School Secretary for 26 years, but echoed by others.

Merstham Primary School entered its post war phase in the hands of some very local staff: Doris **Cox** had been born in Merstham, daughter of Bill Cox, the village postman. Doris had attended the school in the 1930s, going on to a teacher training course in Chichester, before returning to become assistant mistress at the school in 1946. In 1967 she became Deputy Head on Mrs. Stribbling's retirement, and served in this position until her own retirement in 1985, after almost 40 years' service to the school. Mr. A. E. C. (Charles) **Agate** was born in Frenches Road, Redhill, and first took up a teaching job in Leatherhead in 1928. He joined the RAF for the 1939-45 War, opting to be one of the first parachute trainers. He had an active war (being awarded the Air Force Cross) and ended up in the Guinness Book of Records for a record 1,601 jumps. Returning to teaching he was soon appointed headmaster of the Primary School in 1952 at a critical moment in its history. The new estate had been built for the London County Council and was not part of Surrey County's responsibility. From 1954 it had its own Infant School (Albury Manor) in Sunstone Grove presided over by Misses Gill and Warren, and its own Primary Schools, Furzefield in Delabole Road for those North of Bletchingley Road run by Mr. Pratt, and Albury Manor on Taynton Drive for those South of Bletchingley Road, run by Mr. Gibson. Norman Worsfold recalls how strict Mr. Gibson and Miss Jarmen were but, as he puts it, "what wonderful pupils they turned out"! In order to ensure the full use of Furzefield and Albury Schools, a zoning order was introduced to stop children from the estate attending Merstham Primary School and this remained in place until the mid '60s. Rivalry and some ill-feeling between the schools was bound to follow and Mr. Agate had to cope with these pressures as well as the increasing demands of his own education authority. In particular when, in 1969, it closed the Junior section of the school, against the wishes of staff and parents. It was "Merstham First School" until the 1994 reorganisation restored its full Primary School status. But Charles Agate was too old to stay on for that – he retired in 1970 aged 65.

Entertainment, sport and social influences

The London theatre has a long tradition going back centuries. At the turn of this century it was dominated by Gilbert & Sullivan's most popular shows. But every form of comedy was in demand, and the Gaiety Company provided the d'Oyly Carte with the main competition for having the longest running shows. The principal actor at the Gaity was young Seymour **Hicks**, who had married another rising star, Ellaline **Terriss**, in 1893. He was the son of an army officer, she the daughter of a successful actor and with a brother in the same trade. The young couple had a hectic time developing their talents and were at the Vaudeville Theatre in 1902 when they landed the leading roles in J.M. Barrie's *Quality Street* which ran for 459 performances (a very long run for those days, and more than *The Pirates of Penzance*) and the settings for which had been done by Edward Lutyens. After the loss of her first child, Ellaline had been told she could not expect another, so the arrival of Betty was very special to her. It was shortly after this that they bought Cromwell Cottage, or The Old Forge as it was renamed (Cromwell was hardly an appropriate association for actors, and Catholic ones at that), just outside the gates to Merstham House, Lord Hylton's seat. It caused the comment "Ah, now all the *quality* live here!" which is how this end of the High Street became known as Quality Street. Apart from acting, Seymour was a playwright (some 64 in all) and stage manager. They were the first to do a tour of the front for the troops in the First World War, and were later to do a number of American tours after that war. They were, however, also very much part of the village and Ellaline was a popular supporter of village fetes, pageants and such like entertainment, and clearly an influence on those, such as the Jarchows, who later established the Merstham Operatic and Dramatic Society. During a break from their wartime Flanders tours, one of their star protégés, Ivy St. Helier, sang at Merstham School, making a lifetime memory for the young pupils. Although the Hicks left Merstham in the late 1920s for a spate of other homes, Ellaline wrote that The Old Forge was "the dearest of them all". It was the house in which she brought up her daughter. Seymour was knighted in 1935 and Macintosh then introduced its toffee and chocolate assortment, *Quality Street*, for 6d a quarter, a favourite still, though Macintosh has long been absorbed into Rowntree and that company into

Merstham pageant 1920

Rev. John Stonehouse and Eileen Johnson
with the Childrens fancy dress party, Coronation 1953

Nestlé. Sir Seymour Hicks died in 1949 but his widow lived just beyond her 100th birthday in 1971. Their daughter, Betty, had also followed an acting career, married Willie Spillane, a South African, and settled elsewhere in Surrey.

Another name very well remembered from this inter-war period was that of Willy **Smith**. Willy was born in 1872 and lived in Merstham through to 1969. He went to school in the old village School House in what is now Quality Street, and took over his father's shoe repair business in the High Street. But that is not what he is best remembered for. He and his wife, Lilian, were expert dancers, who taught most of the young of the village at that time, and could still show them a thing or two well into old age. Willy's other expertise was as a cricketer at a time when there was a lot of competition, especially locally (Surrey heading the counties' lists). His first game for Merstham Cricket Club was in 1883 when he was 11 years old, at a time when the Club prepared the pitch with scythe, fagging hook, stone roller and a wooden beater to get rid of the hoof dents! In the millennium year of 1900 he scored 600 runs and took 74 wickets and this was typical of him. In 1905 he topped 1,000 runs for the first time and went from strength to strength. From then on he was also coach to a number of young beginners both locally and, for the next two years, at Alleyn's School in Dulwich. He said that his best matches were from 1910-1914, netting 500 runs in one Cricket Week. After the First World War, he was one of the main influences in founding the Merstham Village Club for the men returning to civilian life. During the inter-war period, he was also leader of the Happy Six dance band; he played double bass, while his son, Russell, played the piano. He is remembered by generations of Merstham folk as a very positive influence on the life of the village. Russell was also a cricketer, not surprisingly. Cricket was a remarkably unifying influence in the village. The team was almost completely drawn from people living or working in the village and the Cricket Week referred to was the social high point of the village, teas being provided originally by the well-to-do families, and served by their maids in full uniform! After the depression of 1930/1, the teas were increasingly provided by the players' wives, but it remained a focal point of village life, regardless of rank.

The other main community sport is football and the Merstham Football Club was founded before the start of the century, in 1892, when Mr. Nicol had just started developing

South Merstham, the quarry line had not been built and the village school was still in what is now Quality Street. Indeed, sports were not part of the school curriculum until 1906, so there must have been some very keen local players to have the club established so soon. In the 1920s the Stephens gave 5 acres of Coppice Lea's farm lands to the then local authority to form a recreation ground beside Albury Road and the football club has played there ever since. The club has always been well supported by the community and early on became an affiliate of the Surrey region of the Football Association. In 1964 it self-financed the facilities building beside Albury Road. Twenty years later, it built a club house on Weldon Way (opened by Fulham F.C.) and, a decade after that, it set up its present floodlights (opened by Crystal Palace F.C.). It now has 300 members and runs teams for every age group, including the popular mini football for boys and girls. However, its 34-year-old facilities are now the worst in Surrey and it is regularly fined by the F.A. as a result. Although planning consent for a proper facilities stand has been given by the borough, there was no funding available to do the job at the time of writing.

In 1907 Baden-Powell had started the Boy Scouts movement and it had grown dramatically. When the formal Boy Scouts Association was set up, its first Vice President was Sir Jeremiah Colman of Gatton. It is therefore not surprising that it was so well supported locally. Newton **Hazel** set up a Merstham troop in 1909, two years before setting up another one for Reigate. He was manager of Lloyds Bank (there was a sub-branch in Merstham High Street though Hazel was with the Redhill branch) and living with his parents at 11 Devon Road. His brother Lt. Col. Albert Hazel was killed just after the end of the First World War in which his sister Stella also served as a FANY (volunteer nurse). She used to tell how she had to leave the ambulance after helping with an operation because the sight of blood made her sick! One of Newton Hazel's colleagues in the early years was young Courtenay Woodhouse and, when he joined the war's Roll of Honour, his sister Rosamund took up the role of Cub mistress, making a more lasting memorial to her brother's adventurous spirit that any stone inscription. After the death of their parents in the '20s, Newton and his sister Stella built "Harwell", now 7 Devon Road, with a garden big enough to accommodate the house and two bungalows that were erected in it after their departure in the '50s. The brother and sister were key supporters of All Saints Church throughout their time in the parish, and, as an ARP colleague of Ron Shaw's, Newton was "stationed" at the Church during the Second World War. Newton Hazel also represented the area as councillor on the Reigate RDC and, in this capacity, was part of the early morning group that witnessed Fred Prevett of Albury Road pass over the 1948 Olympic Torch to the next runner as part of the traditional starting procedure for the Games.

The cinema rapidly took over from the theatre as the main indoor entertainment early in this century and the nearest to Merstham were a couple in Redhill, before the Odeon was built in what is now a night club (*The Embassy*). The Picture House in Station Road (since rebuilt as the Arcade) was owned by Mr. Thompson who lived in Hazelton, in Battlebridge Lane, on the Eastern side of the railway. He was remarkable to his neighbours at the time for going around in a coat with an astrakhan collar. His cook, Rosie, doubled up as the box office cashier in his cinema, recycling the boxes of chocolate bought for her from the usherette by her numerous admirers!

Within the village, the annual Fair was the major family occasion. The right for the village to hold this event every 17th September was established by a medieval charter[12] and the date was well known to the travelling Fair folk who would duly turn up in their horse-drawn caravans for the day. On a given signal, there would be a rush by them to get the best sites on the High Street/Quality Street. For the rest of the day they would sell entertainment and goodies primarily to the children for whom the day was as important as Christmas and birthdays. In these pre-multimedia days, there was great entertainment value to be derived from hoop-la, roll-a-penny, coconut shies, fortune telling stalls and merry-go-rounds. It would get into full swing at night with flares lit along the street (the residents would board up their windows). By the morning of 18th it was all over and the caravans had moved on. In the 1930s the residents of Quality Street had the venue moved initially to a field that used to be on the corner of Rockshaw Road (hence Fairfield Cottages) and then to a field rented by Mr. Joyce the butcher in what is now Bushett's Grove. Apart from home-made "humbugs" and water squirters, it was the bonfire-cooked potatoes – sometimes carried home in wads of newspaper – that were the most memorable. The last such Fair was in 1938 as the authorities would not permit it during the Second World War,

---

[12] The 1338 charter was granted by King Edward III to the prior of Canterbury, who owned Merstham at the time, and originally stipulated June 17th as the appropriate day.

MADS triumph 1951 (Mackie Green, Geoffrey Martell, Joy Anderson, Cecile Hummel, Denise Pearse and George Robertson)

Merstham carnival 1960s

the charter rights thus lapsing. Its successor, the Quality Street Fayre, was originally the St. Katharine's Fayre, set up by Rev. Philip Duval in his Rectory grounds in July 1979. From there it spilled over to Quality Street and took on some of the character of the pre-war fairs. This was due to the strenuous organisational skills of Elizabeth and John Callow, who officially retired as chief organisers in 1996, but are still very much part of it.

The Merstham Amateur Dramatic Society (MADS) had been a thriving little group in the 1930s, presenting on average two full productions a year, including the occasional one-act plays that it entered for the Betchworth Drama League Festival, of which it had been a co-founder. In those pre-television days, local drama productions were a staple part of any organisation (W.I., Youth Club and schools), but the MADS' productions were *the* social event of the local calendar at the time. However, in 1939, the Society's activities lapsed when several of its members were conscripted into active service. Luckily the remaining members found an energetic producer to ensure that it was resurrected post-war: Mrs. Joy **Anderson** lived at Eglinton on Church Hill and early in the war had organised a concert given by the Merstham Girls Club in the Village Hall. From this club she created a local branch of the Women's Junior Air Corps, with training provided by Mr. Charlesworth, a former Guards sergeant, and an allotment in which they were to "dig for victory". It was not all hard work: For example, it was not unusual for the Corps girls to be taken to a dance at Smallfield Hospital by their Canadian Army visitors. Joy was widowed in 1943 and from then on put all her energies into drama, producing *Once Upon a Time* in 1943, and J. M. Barrie's *Quality Street* in 1944, with an all-girl cast. The following year she put on her own play, *The Red Campbells*, especially for her Junior Air Corps girls, prior to their being disbanded. In March 1947, she presented three performances of *Ever After* by Nicholas Penny (the leading lady, Sonia Bowring, became engaged during the rehearsals). It was a great success, which was just as well as it turned out that "Nicholas Penny" was Joy's *nom de plume*! As a result of that, she was invited by Sir Harold Webbe and Charles Copper to re-form MADS with herself as producer. In effect it had been a MADS production anyway and the Society's records includes it as its first post war production. She quickly imbued the amateur team with a strongly professional approach and MADS became well known for the high standard of its productions. There have been over 100 post war MADS productions, virtually all in the Village Hall, to an audience of up to 200 people, and with an orchestra that would dress up for the occasion. One of its high points was in 1951 when it won the Kate Rorke Cup and competed in the Area Finals of the National Festival of Community Drama in London. Another was in 1973 when it won the Divisional Final and the Area Final, narrowly missing the All-England triumph, for its (Denise Kennedy's) production of Shaw's *Epilogue to St. Joan*. When Joy died four years later, "Merstham lost one of its most eminent, gifted and affectionately regarded personalities"[13]. Among the many involved in these high years of MADS was Mrs. Laura **Batchelor** of Wellhead, Gatton Bottom, who contributed to the wardrobe and whose enthusiasm for the performing arts has been passed on to her daughter, Elizabeth Callow. Laura was the organiser of the WI's outings through the '70s, passing on her knowledge and enthusiasm for ballet and the theatre to a generation of local ladies. She would queue all night if necessary to get Covent Garden tickets, and would be as thorough in organising a trip to the TV show *Petticoat Lane* as she was about getting her own family to the ballet in Moscow: "Her unfailing cheerfulness and friendliness made outings something to be remembered"[14].

Among the celebrations for the end of the Second World War, was a street party for Albury and Bourne Roads. With the money left over there, an annual supper was organised and this became a regular event for pensioners organised by the Merstham Peace Commemoration Committee, chaired for 20 years by Albert **Barratt** (Presidents included Miss Hummel and Dr. Tayler). Mr. Barratt was also deputy of the Merstham Community Centre. He and the other committee members did a splendid job in organising the event, every member being responsible for the cooking, transport <u>and</u> the washing up (there were no disposable plates and cutlery, even when such became later available; it was a matter of standards). In the prolonged freeze of 1947, Albert Barratt proposed the use of surplus funds to provide coal to the pensioners of the entire village, and 1 cwt of coal per pensioner was duly distributed. Funding of the supper, however, became progressively difficult and it was only through the collections and raffles organised by Frank Chart and his son Dennis, of *The Griffin* pub on the

---

[13] Guy Bingham, writing in the County Post, Times Herald.
[14] Rosemary Stephens in her history of Merstham WI's first 70 years.

Fred Prevett passing on the 1948 Olympic torch

Messrs. Toms, Williamson, Leadbetter and Redfern with the Youth Club football team 1949

corner of Albury and Southcote Roads, that the event lasted as long as it did. Having originally been held in The Village Hall, it moved to Albury Manor School and only stopped when an arsonist put paid to the venue about 1990. What made this charitable occasion especially different from most, is that it was always drawn from every section of Merstham's communities.

Charlie Wall had a keen young assistant master at Merstham School, Michael Adams, who had set up a Merstham Young Men's Club from the school's old boys in 1941. The Merstham Girls' Club started shortly afterwards and Mr. Wall proposed a "governing committee" which became The Merstham Youth Centre, when the boys and girls clubs were merged in 1944. At this time Adams went into the Navy, leaving the Centre in the capable hands of Sydney **Matthewman**, who had run printing classes for the Club, and his wife, who wrote for Mills & Boon. It was they who negotiated with Lord Hylton for "Broadmead" in Station Road, which had been leased originally to Dr. Barnado's and then had been an evacuation centre during the hostilities. A grant from the Surrey Education Authority was received, which institution also provided a warden, initially part-time, but soon to be the County's first full-time Youth Club leader. This was Ernest "Skip" **Williamson**, who was appointed in October 1945, and immediately organised his members to renovate the dilapidated premises, as well as the usual sporting and social activities. Broadmead was officially opened in 1946 and was soon being hailed as a flagship for Youth Clubs. With the positive support of the committee[15], Skip then moved the Centre, and his family, to Oakley in Radstock Way in 1953 just in time for the LCC development and the arrival of hundreds of families from London. Merstham was not alone in having a bulge in its demographics caused by the post-war baby boom, but it was accentuated by the newcomers to the estate being recently married couples. The number of children was a factor in allocating priority for the housing lists, so it was not surprising, for example, to find there were more than 200 children under the age of 10 in just one street, Chesterton Drive, making an average of over six children per family. The children grew up together, swelling the local schools, keeping the buses, shops and sports fields (and the Odeon cinema in Redhill) busy. Oakley became the focal point for a large number of this young generation, where they got involved in discussion

---

[15] Mr Toms of Rockshaw Road was the chairman, Mr Barratt its vice chairman.

groups, drama sessions, walking trips, the annual fete, etc. at a time when television was still black and white and pirate radio stations the main source of pop music. As they grew up together, so they left home about the same time (the GLC rules made it virtually impossible to get onto the housing lists for the estate in which they had grown up) and by the 1970s there were already complaints that the population of the estate had become too middle-aged. Wates the builders had made an offer for the Oakley grounds and it is a tribute to the then committee members, Roger Constant, Jock Hunter, Philip Duval, Muriel Clarke and Barry Newsome, that the Centre survived. Skip kept the Club going, retiring (to Derbyshire) in 1978, after 32 years in the job. A great number of present parents owe their community values to his Youth club, and it continues as the Merstham Youth & Community Centre still.

One of the country's oldest sports is currently on the wane, so that one forgets how popular boxing used to be. When the Village Hall was not being used for amateur dramatics, dances, auctions, dinners or as a library, it was also the venue for boxing shows which were staged with the help of the Guardsmen from their depot in Caterham, RSM Brittain adjudicating. There was also a boxing demonstration included in All Saints' fete, courtesy of Richard **Hill** of 37 Weldon Way. Richard had been ABA featherweight champion in 1947 and 1948, and he continued to encourage the next generation in his work at a London Boys Club. Locally he also supported the Merstham Newton Football Club, and was an active member of All Saints' activities for over 30 years.

In this review of the century, there has been regular mention of Merstham's Women's Institute, demonstrating how powerful an organisation it has been. Indeed its activities continue to get regular coverage in the weekly *Surrey Mirror*. It was not the first in the area – Battlebridge W.I. claims that honour – nor is it the last. From the late 1960s women were increasingly keeping a job as well as a family, which made it impossible to be involved in the mainly afternoon-oriented activities presented by the Merstham W.I. Accordingly a new, evening-based, Women's Institute was set up in 1970 by 43 ladies of South Merstham, with Canada Hall as its venue. Its drama group developed a life of its own and became "Razzamatazz", the self-supporting light entertainment group, in 1988, taking a number of the then 90-strong members with it. The splendid village map that hangs in the Moat House was the result of a county-wide competition entered by the Canada Hall Women's Institute.

It is difficult to cover all the various forms of entertainment, or the prime entertainers. Pubs, and publicans, though, have been a staple part of the English village scene, whether "tied" to a brewery, or "free". The most historical must be *The Feathers Hotel* which the Jolliffes rebuilt to take advantage of the coach traffic on their new turnpike in the early 19th century. Its current construction dates from 1894 and has been the backdrop of several London-to-Brighton travellers, in veteran cars, on bike, on a big ball[16] or by more ordinary means. Lord Hylton sold it earlier this century to Clarke Baker & Co. and it has changed hands at least once again since. The *Jolliffe Arms* originally served a similar purpose to *The Feathers* in London Road North, though both ceased operating as hotels after the Second World War. Appropriate to the Jolliffe connection with the Battle of the Nile, its landlords were thereafter ex-naval men, first James Duncan who retired to Scotland where he could develop Scottish traditional fiddling, and E. Davey who moved on to run Rookwood House in the early '90s. The *Jolliffe Arms* became briefly *Detroits* theme pub in 1992/3 and was then divided, half being *The Shepherds Pen*, which is back on the market at the time of writing. Almost opposite *The Feathers*, *The Railway Arms*, brewery-owned until acquired by Mercury Taverns[17], is still the nearest to the traditional image of a pub. Of similar, if not earlier, antiquity would have been *The Spotted Cow* in Warwick Wold, briefly renamed the *Warwick Arms*, before disappearing beneath the new M23/M25 interchange. Another short-lived pub was *The Cottage of Content*, at the Southern corner of the High Street, which was converted to a private house by Jim Oliver. *The Griffin* was South Merstham's pub, being initially extended from an original house and then completely rebuilt as *The Limes* currently. Finally there is *The Iron Horse* tavern on the corner of Bletchingley Road and Portland Drive, built in 1956. Taken together, they chart the expansion of the village and its social drinking habit through to the 1980s when the drink/driving laws have increasingly curtailed their casual use, especially those sited on the A23, with *Gatton Point* being the latest casualty, being bulldozed in 1998.

---

[16] Mary Morris mentions in her History the lady (p. 67) who was lifted off her ball for refreshment in the Feathers, and then back on it, to ensure she should win her bet that she would get to Brighton without her feet touching the ground.
[17] Acquired by Pubmaster Ltd. in June '98, who awarded its publican Linda Lewis top honours for its décor theme.

For those of a more sober disposition, there were a number of tea rooms and restaurants, of which Quality Café (Mrs. Bateman) in Station Road has proved the most enduring. For a while, it had been rivalled by The Golden Wheel Restaurant (Mrs. Thurston) at the top of School Hill, though this ceased being a restaurant in the 70s. Opposite, in The Old Saddlery, Peter and Ruth Hamlin were responsible for entertaining the mind rather than the stomach: He made organs, she was a professional pianist. Reverting to entertainers, Ted **Wicks** came to Merstham in 1937 and ran a band, "Ted Wix and his Music", that was popular locally. During the war, when on leave from the RAF, he would play for dances in the Village Hall. After the war he performed regularly at the Market Hall in Redhill. More recently, from the late '70s, Mr. Newton set up Potters in the High Street, one of the few violin makers in the region. For those who preferred using their voice rather than an instrument, there were, and are, a number of choral and operatic societies based in Redhill and Reigate. Merstham's own opera singer was **Nora Gruhn** who had retired to a house on Beech Road which she renamed "Warble Hatch". She ran a little opera group which, among other events, entertained The Merstham Society in 1965. Somewhat later, Merstham became the home of Sir Arthur **Davison**, best remembered for his concerts, aimed primarily for children, conducted at Fairfield Hall in Croydon. He had started them in 1966, following a period of being director and deputy leader of the London Philharmonic Orchestra. Following his divorce and marriage to his second wife in 1978, he moved to Glencairn on Shepherds Hill. He was already 60 at the time and had passed on the running of his children's concerts to his son, Darrell. He died in 1992. Doubtless there are plenty of other Merstham entertainers honing their skills for the new century.

Farmers and forces servicemen

Only a fraction of Merstham parish is farmed these days, but there were a number of farms at the opening of the century[18]: Joseph Chandler at Albury Farm, Thomas King at Alderstead and Dean Farms, and Harrie **Stacey** who was Lord Hylton's estate manager, which included Home Farm, Boars Green Farm and the ancient Cold Roast Farm that used to be at the top of Harps Oak Lane. The Staceys were a well-established Merstham family, one Michael Stacey being listed as tenant farmer of Home Farm back in the 1830s. Maurice **Stradling** took over the tenancy of Home Farm in 1918 and his grandson still lives in the village. So much of Merstham's farmland has disappeared that it is hard to imagine what a rural community it was originally. There is still Merstham Farm Services Ltd. based next to the former *Jolliffe Arms* (currently *Shepherds Pen*), and its predecessor was a similar business – renting out threshing machines – carried out by Mr. **Stribbling** of Albury Road. Mr. Stribbling was a "huge 20 stone" man, whose collection of traction engines were in much demand, not just locally but also on the Continent. He was also captain of Merstham's volunteer Fire Brigade, which had a hand-cart tender based in a purpose-made building provided by Lord Hylton in Station Road. This was an appropriate location at the time because then there was a water mill to the north of this road (behind the GPO building) that was demolished in the 1930s, long before the motorway was carved through its water source. The redundant windmill that featured in the early postcards of late Victorian Merstham had been dismantled, and its timbers and grindstones used for St. Katharine's new lychgate, dedicated to William Stacey, the parish's last miller. By the time of the First World War, the Stacey family occupation fully reflected the change in land use. The war claimed one of them: Lt. John Stacey started with the East Surrey's, transferring to the Flying Corps shortly afterwards. However, he was killed in action in December 1917. A Frank Stacey farmed Hoath Farm at the junction of Harps Oak Lane and London Road North in the 1930s. Harrie and his wife Sarah moved to Chilberton, Reigate, where he died during another war, in December 1943, aged 85. His firm of estate

---

[18] Battlebridge dairy Farm had lost most of its fields first to the LBSC railway, then to housing, before the turn of the century, though the ancient building was left as an increasingly derelict relic between the railway lines.

agents, Harrie Stacey & Son of Bell Street, was still in business in Reigate, Redhill and Tadworth a decade later.

The Grange, just off London Road South, was the home of the **Roffey** family. One Robert Roffey is mentioned in the *Gentleman's Magazine* in 1830 as an excellent huntsman and was also listed as tenant of Albury Farm and Churchwarden to St Katharine's. By the turn of this century, there was a William Roffey in Chaldon and George Roffey at the Grange, Merstham, with his mother Adah (who was 100 years old when she died in 1912), wife and children: He had two sons, G. Walter and Harold, both of whom had left home for the army: Walter had started with the regulars in 1885, transferred to a TA unit for a few years while he played football for Surrey 1891-5, and then left the army for the grain trade about the time he got married to Constance Laurence in 1897. His brother Harold had seen active service in the Tirah campaign in NW India, and then in the South Africa War 1899-1902. When the First World War started Walter was vice president of the London Corn Trade Association but, after his brother was wounded on the retreat from Mons, joined his brother's regiment, The Lancashire Fusiliers, so that both of them had the same uniform even if very different occupations. Harold was awarded the DSO in 1917, but was killed in action in April 1918 (he is joint senior ranking with Lt. Col. Hazel on the Merstham War Memorial). Walter Roffey received a knighthood, for organising food supplies, and moved to East Grinstead, then Lingfield, but not back to Merstham. There were also two sisters, one of whom, Maud, stayed on at the Grange. She found a kindred spirit in her younger neighbours, Mrs. Lottie Stephens and Ulricho Jarchow. With Lottie, she promoted the suffragette movement; all three founded the Merstham Nursing Association and were obvious founder members of Merstham's Women's Institute, Maud being its second president, for 1920/21. Both Maud and Lottie were to end up prominent, and benevolent, figures in local government and both were to die relatively young at 58 and 56 respectively. Maud had been a "FANY", being trained as a physiotherapist, at Merstham's VAD hospital at Chaldon Rise. When her father died, she moved to Rye, became a Catholic and was elected to the Town Council, from which she conducted a war on poverty and disease. She was a Governor of Rye Grammar School, worked for the Rye Memorial Hospital, was on the Relief Committee of the British Legion and founded Rye's Catholic Church. If it seems somewhat remote from Merstham, it is noticeable that the principal mourners at her funeral in 1932, apart from relatives, were the Stephens, the Jarchows, Paxton Watson and his sister and John West (of Myrtlecroft, Deans Road), all of Merstham.

According to the Rector's records, there were only fields between Wells Nurseries and the new Primary School on London Road South in 1907, and these were rented by Mr. **Dawes**, "a dairyman, for the grazing of cattle with chicken runs, etc.". The Dawes lived at The Limes at the top of School Hill and would employ some of their daughter's school friends to help out in the dairy (now Pear Tree Cottage) beside the house. Mr. Dawes would then deliver milk through the village from his handcart. There was also a dairy at 46 Nutfield Road, run by the Luxtons. By the end of the '30s there were some other competing dairy farmers, another result of the rising village population: Mr. Ron **Shaw** was the son of a dairyman, and a grandson of the Simeon Shaw whose wheelwright's business in the 1840s gave its name to the Shaw's Corner area between Reigate and what became Redhill. Accordingly his education was at St. John's Redhill, where he proved bright enough to go on to the Reigate Grammar School. As expected, he followed his father into the family milk business, but joined the army for the First World War, serving at Ypres and the Somme where he was wounded 3 times, the only permanent damage being deafness in one ear. He was sent to Liverpool hospital to recuperate, where he made friends with a Scotsman from Colinton. Such was their friendship, that he spent a holiday with their family, fell in love with his friend's sister and married her in 1926 (hence his house in Deans Road was named Colinton). In the meantime he had been employed as the school attendance officer ("Just the person we need – he can turn a deaf ear to the lame excuses"!) for Merstham School, a role he took seriously, viewing the employment of under-age children as exploitation. But his vigilance was matched by his kindness to the genuinely ill children he came across. He is also remembered for his service with the ARP Ambulance in the Second World War. He died, aged 91, in 1985 leaving a son and daughter (Ruth, who is still in Merstham) and four grandchildren.

The **Peters** were another well established local family, having been at Quarry Dean Farm, below Shepherds Hill, from which they ran *Greystone Lime Works*, since the mid 19th century. Here the first Peters to take on the quarries had invited young Alfred

Noble to demonstrate his new invention, dynamite, in 1867, to most of the senior extraction engineers of the time. Just before the turn of the century, the second, by-pass, railway tracks were run through their quarries, and their branch line from the quarry was re-connected to this new line. The Peters private engine at this time was called after their son, Gervaise. As with John Stacey, Gervaise Peters joined the Army in the First World War. He survived the Mesopotania campaign, in which he was wounded. At the end of the war, his father was the one who handed out certificates to all Merstham's returning servicemen, a cruel irony as his own son never returned: Gervaise was killed in action on the North West Frontier in India in 1920, aged 24. It cannot be coincidence that the former bakers shop in the High Street was named Gervaise Cottage by the Matthewman family. By then the Peters family was already involved more with farming than minerals, Nancy teaching a number of the local children how to ride (and providing the Reigate Pageants with ponies) in the 1950s. The Peters family moved to Reigate, their farm being taken on by the Harrisons who fought off an attempt in 1960 by Croydon Council to use the quarries as a tip for household waste. In the process Mullens Harrison gave some publicity to the old medieval masons tunnels beneath his fields (rediscovered as a result of subsidence in the heavy rains of Derby Day 1911) though not all the subsequent newspaper stories, such as the one about an underground boat, and being able to walk underground all the way to Bletchingley, have been proved. The Harrisons farmed the smallholding until most of it, the farmhouse included, was compulsorily purchased for the M23. For reasons that may have nothing to do with Tandridge Council's tinkers' camp the other side of the motorway, the former farm track became a dumping ground, especially for torched stolen cars, in the early '90s. Only some untended ancient apple trees remind one that there was once a carefully cultivated living here.

It is obvious that the First World War had a marked impact on this newly growing community and so is not surprising to find the survivors gave a lot of support to the Memorial Fund. The War Memorials at the top of School Hill and beside All Saints were an obvious result (added to after the next war, and renovated in the 1980s), and a Village Hall and Club the next popular choice. But there was some division of opinion as to for whose benefit the proceeds should be. The Merstham branch of the newly formed British Legion (the president at the time being Col. Norman Rolls DSO of Little Shaw, Rockshaw Road) felt they should run it, while the main financial backers felt it should be for the village as a whole. In the end the British Legion built their own meeting place on a site they bought for the special price of £100 in Albury Road, while the Hall & Club were taken on by the Village Trust, set up by a London solicitor, Kenny Birt of Merlebank, Church Hill, former neighbour of Col. Rolls. The ex-Servicemen's Club building, that was also the headquarters of the local British Legion, was erected voluntarily at weekends by the ex-servicemen themselves in 1926 and formally opened in May 1927 in an impressive ceremony attended by the then First Sea Lord and Lady Edward Spencer Churchill. Dr. Weir was the Merstham Legion's president at the time, with Maj. Marshall of Merstham Post Office its chairman. A women's section of the British Legion was quite rare nationally, but Merstham had one with 130 members and Miss Alice M. Stewart of the Old Manor House in Quality Street was its chairman and a most efficient fund raiser. The women's section was disbanded at the end of 1982, at which point 38 former members were recognised as having had a lifelong association with the section. The Royal British Legion, boosted by another World War, lasted several decades on its original site at 10 Albury Road, "held in trust in perpetuity for the benefit of all ex-Servicemen in the Merstham Area". However, times change and in 1994 it was replaced by a smart little estate called Regent Close (it should have been "Poppy Close"). The local branch now uses the facilities of Merstham Football Club on Weldon Way.

Miss Watson, the architect's sister, sold her house on Rockshaw Road, Pickett Wood, to Gen. Sir Walter **Campbell** and his wife, who retired here in 1927 after an active, and distinguished career. He had started off with the Gordon Highlanders and seen action in several Indian and South African campaigns before the turn of the century. After initial service in Flanders in the First World War, he was posted to the Gallipoli beachhead, where he made such an impressive job of securing the retreat with minimum casualties that he was taken onto Allenby's staff in time for his rapid advance through Palestine and Syria. By 1918, Campbell was responsible for maintenance in the field of over a quarter of a million men and their animals. Life was somewhat dull thereafter. He was described as having a "strong personality, with some obstinacy in its composition; when he made up his mind, nothing would

defeat him", though "he never bore anyone any ill-will, and disliked intensely any form of publicity or self-advertisement. His real happiness was always to be found with his family and friends".[19] He died, aged 72, in 1936 and his wife stayed on in the house for two more years. After a brief period of ownership by Sir John Anderson, their house was later purchased by another General.

Sir David **Lambert** DSO was the son of an army general, but joined the Navy at 18 in 1903. He had served throughout the First World War in the Royal Canadian Navy, marrying Dorothy Jones from Victoria, BC in Canada in 1920. They had no children. He was appointed Paymaster Captain in 1934 and moved first on to Hill Top Lane at the Chaldon end of the village and later The Red House on Rockshaw Road. With the rapid replenishment of the armed forces following the Munich agreement, he was promoted to Paymaster Director General with the rank of Paymaster Rear Admiral. It was a traumatic time to be at the War Office and he would have been relieved to retire in May 1942. Although he was a typical gentleman of the old school, it was his wife, Lady Lambert, who was better known for her social capabilities ("a good mixer"). She was president of the WI for 1951/2 when, in the context of the sudden increase in local population, it voted to limit membership to a maximum of 175. The separate Canada Hall W.I. of South Merstham was formed later, in 1970.

Merstham was not peculiar in housing a large number of representatives of the services. Apart from the traditional needs of a country that for most of the century had to police most of the world, both World Wars required conscription of most able-bodied men of the time. So it is only recent generations that need not expect to don uniform. Typical of a generation entering this century, J. H. **Green** got caught up in the First World War, less typically earning a commission from the ranks in 1915 (aged only 22) and was wounded just before that war's end. Given the prejudice of the time against those who had risen from the ranks, he transferred to the Indian Army and was appointed to the newly formed Burma Rifles. After being involved in the Malibar campaign, he was appointed Captain in charge of recruitment in Burma – he spoke the language by then

[19] Quoted in his obituary in *The Times* 12 Aug. 1936

Victory parade, High Street, 1945

– and went on to serve in the Burma campaign of 1931-32 for which he was mentioned in despatches, promoted to Major, and awarded the MBE. His service record is pertinent because, on retiring to Shepherds Hill, Merstham, after the Second World War, his interest in his regiment was such that his widow, Dorothy, was engaged in making a Burma Rifles regimental museum out of an annex to Southfields after his death. She died in 1994 before it could be officially completed or sanctioned. It is interesting to think of Merstham being the unlikely venue for such a piece of Imperial history.

Of much the same generation, Charles **Morris** was a typical freshly commissioned 19 year old Lieutenant when he joined the Western Front in 1917. The following year he was posted to the Balkan front (Salonika) where he was wounded, being nursed there by, among others, Rosamond Woodhouse, daughter of Merstham's rector, whom he married. His regiment was the Indian Frontier Rifles and he went on to see active service in Waziristan and the North West Frontier for which, in 1938, he was awarded his DSO. They had four children who, typical of overseas forces families, also spent a lot of time with their aunt, Helen Woodhouse, in The Cottage, Quality Street. Eventually Maj. Morris acquired Merlebank in Church Hill as a stable base for his family, just in time for the next World War. He was promoted Colonel of his regiment and was soon involved in the North African campaign. There is a story told about his temporary capture by the Germans there[20] but his son says it was exaggerated for propaganda purposes. His regiment did find itself cut off behind enemy lines in the highly fluid movements before Alamein in 1942 and was certainly able to extricate itself only through a certain amount of decisive bluff on the part of Col. Morris. In the partition of India following the war, his regiment was naturally transferred to the new state of Pakistan which was a bitter blow to its British officers. He was only 51 at his death in 1950. His interest in history was shared by his wife, Rosamund, who gave an excellent talk on "Merstham Memories" in 1957, an interest passed on to the next generation, who published Merstham's favourite history book. At the end of 1962, Mrs. Morris retired from the scout movement after 50 years of service (apart from the times she was overseas) to the Merstham cubs. She was particularly proud of having kept the pack going through both world wars. When

---

[20] As reported by the papers, and duly included in Compton Mackenzie's *Eastern Epic*

VE Day street party, Albury Road

VE Day street party, Brook Road

her sister Helen died in 1966, she and her children took over her Quality Street house. Mrs. Morris died three years later; Mary and Coutenay are still very much part of the community, Courtenay being secretary of The Merstham Society from 1979 to 1997.

Another officer who saw service in both world wars arrived in Merstham for his retirement. Maj-Gen. Frederick **Hilton-Sergeant** was another teenager when he was commissioned into the Royal Horse Artillery in 1917, against the wishes of his family. Following the war, he completed his medical studies at university and then transferred into the RAMC, qualifying as an army doctor with flying colours in 1923. From then on he served in India, China and the Middle East, becoming Director of Preventive Medicine for the 8th Army in war-time Egypt. He achieved his final rank in 1953 with promotion to Commandant and Director-General of medical studies, RAMC, at the splendid piece of architecture next door to the Tate Gallery. He was awarded his CBE in 1955, and his CB just before he left the army in 1957 to become medical advisor to the British Red Cross. It was at this time that he and his wife moved to Pickett Wood on Rockshaw Road where they lived until the motorway compulsory purchase took them to Home Cottage in Quality Street. General Hilton-Sergeant died in 1978 but his wife, Kathleen, celebrated her 90th birthday as this was being written.

The immediate need for agricultural produce during the war dropped off as, once again, cheaper imported foodstuffs became available. Given the development of South Merstham, it is surprising to find Edmund Bristow still farming the remaining fields of Battlebridge Farm in the 1950s. Lord Hylton, though, was still the main landowner, with four of the other local farms. At the top of Harps Oak Lane, Cold Roast Farm had suffered from enemy action and was demolished (the same fate as Merstham House after six years friendly occupation), its lands being consolidated with those of Boars Green Farm. Alex **Maiklem** was the farmer of these lands, being additionally responsible for the pheasant woodland ("Furzefield Shaw") that used to extend from the farm to the top of Ashstead Hill until the late 80s. Maurice Stradling still ran Hylton's Home Farm opposite *The Feathers*, as he does to this day, though his grandson Colin has moved on to Rockshaw Road. Alderstead Farm, at the top of Shepherds Hill, was run by Edmund Webber and, below him, Mr. Harrison kept Quarry Dean Farm going, though the farm buildings disappeared under the M23 in 1975. Once both motorways were built the other Merstham and Gatton farming lands (apart from Home Farm) were sold off to form their present relationship between Colebrooke and Mac Maiklem. Fanny Maiklem, daughter-in-law of Alex Maiklem, set up her Farm Shop on Markedge Lane in 1978 and, more recently, has reached a wider audience through her Saturday slot on BBC Southern Counties radio. The main changes to local farming, though, have been the size of field and nature of their contents. Farming has had to take advantage of the benefits of scale to survive, so that a number of smaller fields were consolidated into bigger ones. At the same time there have been changes in EU crop subsidies, so that suddenly the colour of the surrounding fields can become bright yellow with Rape, or pale blue with Linseed, crops that one never saw before the last two decades.

   The need for armed forces also declined dramatically after the Second World War, though it was not immediately obvious in the early phases of the "Cold War". With the abolition of National Service in 1960, the post war Merstham generation has happily not been forced into uniform, though there have still been occasional needs for the smaller professional army to maintain the country's commitments. Such was the conflict over the Argentinean occupation of the Falkland Islands in 1982. At the conclusion of this brief but, nevertheless, nerve-wracking affair, a large tree near Taynton Drive was suitably decked out in yellow ribbon to welcome home Stuart Bush who had served with the Navy there. He went on to serve in the Gulf conflict of 1991, but has never forgotten the welcome home party he received then.

Government members

Merstham has never been statistically significant to national government (the Orbital Motorway route decision being one result), though it should be for local government: In terms of a local constituency, the combined Merstham parishes consisted of only 2,014 people (57% in South Merstham) according to the 1901 census. But by 1931 it had more than doubled, to 4,495, excluding the Netherne patients. This was the size of the responsibility of the Merstham Parish Council until 1933 when the Surrey Review Order transferred the growing hamlet of Hooley in Merstham's northern strip to Banstead Urban District Council (including Netherne Hospital), and the rest was taken over by Reigate Rural District Council. The two boroughs were united to form the present Reigate & Banstead Borough Council in 1974, by which time the estate had increased the Merstham population to about 7,500[21].

The parish councillors were initially more representatives of their parish than members of a political party. Merstham's councillors in 1917, for example, were: G. Hunt, H. de Carteret, W. Willmott, J. J. Pink, and R . P. Sellon, and one cannot judge from the minutes whether they were Conservative, Liberal or Labour. Nationally, the Conservatives were in power from 1915 to 1964 apart from brief interludes in 1924, 1929-31 and 1945-51 but, throughout this period, Merstham's representatives were still more local leaders than political representatives. The following list is not 100% accurate but is a "best effort" to show which *local* councillors sat for the Merstham wards of the borough:

Appointed		Address
1933	Mrs. Ruth Weir	The Bell House, London Road South
,,	Sydney Francis	London Road North
,,	R. E. Shott	Hillside, Church Hill
1935	S. Thomas Pink	181 Nutfield Road
1937	E. Newton Hazel	Harwell, Devon Road
1945	Fred Lilley	107 Nutfield Road
1947	George H. Searle	27 Orpin Road
1949	John I. Quihampton	Hillside, Bletchingley Road

[21] Exact comparisons are difficult – the smaller area of the borough's HA, IA, IB & IC groups had 7,158 in '97.

Appointed		Address
1950	Jock Hunter	Tanglewood, Rockshaw Road
1952	Eileen Johnson	84 Nutfield Road
1955	Tim H. Alleyn	The Old Saddlery, London Road South
1955	Anthony Donovan	13 Weldon Way
1956	William Chapman	47 Malmestone Avenue
1959	'Bert Monger	199 Radstock Way
1961	Sidney C. Oelman	65 Bletchingley Road
1967	John J. Mold	Markedge Lane
1968	R. Norman Heslop	The Corner House, Church Hill
1984	Muriel Clarke	Radstock Way
1986	Barry Newson	Radstock Way
1986	Stephen Seager	Rockshaw Road
1990	Muriel Moore	Crossways
1991	Mark Simpson	lived in Reigate, but ran a protective clothing business in Endsleigh Road
1992	Phil Hitchins	North Lodge, Gatton Bottom

Of these, some of the early ones have been mentioned elsewhere. Fred **Lilley** ran a grocers business in Nutfield Road. In his youth, he had gone off to fight the Fascists in the Spanish Civil War. Such was the impression he made, that he was invited back to Spain by his former comrades once Franco died, in 1975. However, it was only after the death of his wife that he had the time to spare and made the trip back to the scene of his most formative years. Both Tim Alleyn and George Searle were Mayors of Reigate borough for a couple of years each. George **Searle** MBE was mayor for 1957–1959, but this was by no means his only claim to fame: He was president of The Merstham Society from 1963 until his death in 1980, and of The Merstham Amateur Dramatic Society, as well as being on the boards of Albury Manor, Redstone and Furzefield Schools. He himself left school for work at Bryant & May Ltd., the match makers, at 14 just after the First World War, moving on to become eventually director of food transport for the Ministry of Food. His was the generation that knew the 1930's depression first hand and it left on him an indelible concern for all sections of the community. He was just over 40 when he became a local councillor, mayor a decade later, and thus well past retirement age when he retired in 1979, at which point he was appointed honorary alderman of the borough. He took up his ex-officio position as a magistrate in 1959, in which capacity he would always wear a red carnation. In all his roles he was disciplined, capable, conscientious and kind, but also a quiet person who rarely talked about himself. Dudley Bull described him as "one of our leading citizens who tried to make Merstham more than just an anonymous part of the borough".

More recently, political parties have stamped their mark on candidates to a greater extent. When one of the new arrivals to the LCC estate, Mrs. Muriel **Clarke**, a small Welsh lady who had served in the WAAFs throughout the war, wanted to do more for the community, she "thought the Liberal Party was the best party on the local level, one that would listen to people's problems and do more for the individual"[22]. It took several years to convince the electorate of the North East Ward, but she was finally elected by a margin of 18 votes in 1984. She battled on as the only Liberal councillor with such infectious enthusiasm that she captured 50% of the vote at the next opportunity and was no longer the only representative of her party in the borough. It was the deafness of one of her two daughters that gave her a deep interest in, and sympathy for, those with a handicap of any sort. Her warm, caring personality made her a popular and respected person in every activity she undertook. Apart from being secretary of the Reigate Welsh Society, she was active in running the deaf school in Nutfield Priory, the Merstham Youth Centre at Oakley, Merstham Ladies Club, Age Concern and the 66 Club. It was a shock to the community as a whole when, at the end of 1990, she died of cancer at 66 years old.

At a different level, there is the County Council, responsible for Merstham's schools and library. As far as can be judged, the first local to sit on this body was Peter Smalley MBE, an accountant who was briefly in London Road North before retiring to the West Country. Barry **Newsome**, who lived near the junction of Bletchingley Road and Radstock Way, represented Merstham as another Liberal Democrat on the Borough Council, and went on to the County Council, before leaving the village. He is remembered as a charming person, unafraid of work, and of particular support to the Merstham Aid Project. At present, Daniel **Kee**, a lawyer with Noble Lowndes, from Lowood on Rockshaw Road sits as a Conservative member on the County Council, having been its Vice Chairman for 1996-7.

[22] As per her daughter, Mrs Anita Fletcher, quoted in the Surrey Mirror, 20th December 1990.

The City of London has a constitution that pre-dates Parliament, and is still run by its medieval Livery Companies, the senior ones of which are best known for their charitable and educational foundations. One of the families associated over a period of time with the Mercers' Company were the Watneys, of Watney Mann & Co, the brewers. Sir John Watney had married one of the co-heiresses to the Sanders estates and had comfortably brought up three sons at Shermanbury House in Reigate before this century. The eldest died in 1896, leaving Col. Sir Frank Watney to become Clerk to the Mercers Company from 1919 to 1940. Stephen **Watney** was the youngest of the brothers and was Master of the Company in 1920. He would appear to have moved with his wife into Merstham in the '30s on his retirement from the City. Chaldon Rise, at the end of Rockshaw Road, had served as Merstham's Voluntary Aid Detachment (a hospital billet) in the First World War, and so would have been big enough to serve as a home base for Stephen and Sybil, their son, Capt. John Watney of the Rifle Brigade, and their grandchildren. Stephen died there in 1954, aged 85, and his son took a house in Itchenor, Sussex, but the grandson, Christopher, was local enough to end up marrying Patsy Lachelin from just up the road, in 1960. Chaldon Rise is once again a nursing home.

Given the major impact that the London County Council was to have on Merstham, it is fitting that one of its Chairmen, and one that was most concerned for the Green Belt, should have lived here. Harold **Webbe** had had an interesting career. He started off as a teacher and became a Schools' Inspector in 1910. With the outbreak of the First World War he joined the Ministry of Munitions, leaving them for a new career in financial services, becoming chairman of what became Mercantile Credit, a hire purchase company (later part of the Barclays Bank group). In 1925 he became a member of the LCC (later Chairman of its Education Committee) and had Ash Pollard built as his residence at the eastern end of Rockshaw Road. He was a man of substance, though not unduly status-conscious: He would have been "middle aged" when he personally dug out the deep pit needed for his swimming pool. Such was his faith in the Bulls that he was one of the first to supply the new Hawthorns school with boys, both his sons, John and Brian, attending in 1927. Meanwhile, the massive ribbon development that spread out from London's road and rail links threatened communities and amenities that up until then had hardly changed in a century. It was the LCC that proposed the Green Belt Scheme in 1933, and Harold Webbe was head of one of the two parties vying for control, losing out to Herbert Morrison's landslide victory in 1934. Such was the influence of those who had a vested interest in suburban development that it took five years to get the Green Belt regulations onto the statute books, by which time the prospect of another major war was looming. He became Sir (William) Harold Webbe in 1937 and took the old Westminster Abbey seat in the House of Commons from 1939 until just after the War. He was one of those who ensured MADS was resurrected after the war, being its president for those post-war years. He never lost his interest in education and was chairman of the Independent Schools' Association in 1963/4 at the time when the newly elected Labour government posed a major challenge to the private sector. Of his three children, Brian Webbe was with Massey Ferguson, the tractor makers and, with his wife, lived at The Old Forge in Quality Street. While here he took on the chairmanship of the Merstham Protection Society that fought an expensive battle to have the proposed M25 motorway relocated away from the village, though to no avail. The couple were divorced, but later remarried (to each other) and are now Jersey resident. Sir Harold's daughter, Rosemary, married Anthony Stephens in 1941.

More recently, another Merstham resident made the transition from local to central civil service. Anne **Poole** of Church Hill was promoted from being Surrey's Area Nursing Officer in 1981 to being first Deputy Chief Nursing Officer of the DHSS and, from 1982 to 1992, Chief Nursing Officer of that Government Department. She was awarded the DBE on retiring from that post, at which point she became a director of the Area Health Authority (her husband, John, had been chairman) and a Trustee of the Marie Curie Foundation. At an age when most would enjoy retirement, she has since become a member of the Criminal Injuries Compensation Panel, a busy role covering the whole country.

When Britain entered the Second World War, one of the main concerns, with the Spanish Civil War fresh in the mind, was the need to have a secure home front. To deal with this, Chamberlain brought back to England Sir John **Anderson** who had made a strong impression in Bengal, at the time a hotbed of political agitation, and appointed him Home Secretary and Minister of Home Security. John Anderson was a widower with two children at the time and bought Picket Wood in Rockshaw Road from Lady Campbell (possibly on a tip-off from Dick White) as his base. He carried out a number of immediate defence initiatives, of which a relatively less important one was to commission the curved-corrugated-iron-based garden shelter that bears his name. Churchill recognised his qualities and when, in 1940, he took over as Prime Minister, he appointed Sir John as Lord President of the Council, arbitor in effect, of the country's most sensitive decision making. In September 1943, Churchill's physician recorded: "The PM is shocked to read of the sudden death of the Chancellor of the Exchequer, Sir Kingsley Wood, with whom he had been on very friendly terms. Sir John Anderson, the Lord President of the Council, who is now to become Chancellor, is a very different man. There has indeed been nothing quite like him in the Civil Service. His astonishing efficiency depends on an unusual combination of qualities. In the first place, he has an appetite for facts, which he has indulged freely for many years, so that it is almost impossible to catch him out in anything. This grip on detail is reinforced by 'the gift of instinctive judgement'. Anderson only speaks from the bench. To this catalogue of virtues I must add his immense experience of administration and his shining moral courage, which Winston calls 'Sir John's fine spirit'. The Prime Minister has need of such a man: Absorbed himself in the conduct of operation, he has been happy to leave the Home Front to Anderson; he knew nothing would go wrong. A special committee – the most important of all the Cabinet Committees, the PM used to call it – was set up to supervise all matters on this front, with Anderson as Chairman. Sir John was thought by some to be censorious, but he felt he had the right to be critical. The world, after all, had accepted him as a great man, and he saw no reason to demur. I remember once saying to him 'Winston is hopeless with strangers'. He agreed, but added in his pontifical manner, 'Winston must not only get to know a man, he must also find him congenial' and Sir John permitted himself a slight smirk. He would indeed have been pained if he had known that his own solid gifts were not those to set the PM's mind on fire. Winston trusted him, he respected his judgement but he did not always find him congenial"[23]. Not surprisingly, then, Sir John Anderson played little part in the Merstham community. He

[23] From *Winston Churchill, the struggle for survival 1940 – 1965* (1966) by Lord Moran

had his own petrol pump installed at Picket Wood – no rationing for him! After the war, he was elevated to the peerage, as Lord Waverley, and retired to Sussex. In 1952 he had been asked by Churchill to be part of his Government, but turned it down. He was then over 70, and held sufficiently remunerative posts which he could not afford to exchange for a minister's income of £4,000 a year.

When Sir John Anderson took on his 1939 role as Minister of Home Security, one of his most important departments would have been MI5, the clandestine section of Military Intelligence responsible at the time primarily for identifying and defeating Nazi, and Communist, attempts to have effective spy operations in England. One of the professional triumvirate who ran the department before the war was Dick **White** who lived, as a bachelor, in Wood Cottage which was conveniently just below what became Anderson's house. Among other operations, it fell to him to mastermind the deceptions as to the true place and timing of the D-Day landings, for which he was seconded as "expert advisor on counter-intelligence matters" to Eisenhower's staff. He was awarded the American Legion of Merit and the French Croix de Guerre. After the war he married Kate Bellamy and moved to Wisteria Cottage in Quality Street. He was living there when he was promoted, in 1953, to Director General of MI5, at the crucial period of the "Cold War". In 1956 his efficient leadership was recognised by a knighthood and a transfer to become the first civilian head of MI6, and thus the only man to have headed both departments. Just as the pre-war public had an insatiable appetite for books and films on crime, so the post-war public was hooked on secret agents. Sir Dick White was not, however, the role model for Ian Fleming's "M" in his Bond books of the 1960s. His position as Intelligence Coordinator in the Cabinet Office was not easy: Of what is in the public domain, we know he had to contend with the Profumo, Kim Philby and Anthony Blunt affairs. But he had the confidence of both Labour and Conservative ministers who regarded him as a safe pair of hands and valued his advice. Like Sir John Anderson, he "possessed a formidable intellect and a trenchant mind. He would unerringly and instantly identify the central issues and immediately make authoritative proposals to deal with them". Unlike Sir John, "it was not in his nature to be overbearing. He was good company, told a story well, but seldom revealed much about himself. He generated harmony, was always considerate, and never grand with his staff".[24] Sir Dick White sold Wisteria Cottage to Tim Alleyn in 1959, having maintained a suitably low profile throughout the relatively short but vital period he was in Merstham.

After a couple of rebuffs from Gen. de Gaulle, the UK joined the Common Market, as the European Union was then referred to, in 1973. This unelected Commission controlled a structure that was, and is, cumbersome in its numerous directorates and layers, split over the member countries, though principally in Brussels. The creation of a European Parliament, based in Luxembourg, was intended to make the process more democratic, though this century ends without any obvious improvement. That said, it is in keeping with Merstham's remarkable ability to encompass all walks of life to include in its residents a member of the European Parliament. Bob **Battersby** served in Military Intelligence from 1942 to 1947 in Italy, Crete and Macedonia. He then went into engineering sales, becoming increasingly involved with Eastern European plants, in which connection he was appointed advisor to the Eastern European Trade Council 1969-71 and from which he was recruited by GKN to specifically cover that region. He first became involved with the EEC directorates in 1973, so he was a natural candidate for the Conservative Party to field in the European Parliament elections of 1979. True to his county of origin, he was an EMP for Humberside for the subsequent decade. When he was not in Brussels, Luxembourg and other continental venues, though, he returned to his home, initially at Baldwyns in London Road North, and then at West Cross in Rockshaw Road. Members of the Merstham Society were thus able to learn from him a lot more about the realities of the workings of the EEC than was available through the media.

Whatever the level of Government, Merstham has contributed its share of public servants across the political spectrum. The village boasts no clear focal point such as a central village green or major civic amenity. It has been partitioned by railways and motorways, and lacks its name on all its boundaries, and now in its postal address, but it is still home to people who care about such matters of community pride.

---

[24] As quoted in his obituary in *The Times*, 20th February 1993.

Horticulturists

The stream that was the basis of the village's existence for over 1,300 years has all but disappeared as a result of this century's construction work but it, together with its tributary from Gatton, was the reason why some excellent nurseries were sited in the Battlebridge (and Wiggy) area locally. In 1903, 55-year-old Mr. W. **Wells** acquired the farmland to the East of London Road South from Jeremiah Colman and built his greenhouses, the central one being reputed to be the largest in Surrey. Mr. Wells had been head gardener at Worth and in 1877 set up his own chrysanthemum business at Earlswood. It grew rapidly and he moved to South Merstham with a national reputation as a grower and exhibitor of this species of flower. At a time when most of his contemporaries would be looking forward to retirement, he set about making Wells Nurseries internationally known, specialising additionally in carnations from 1910. To keep in touch with the competition, he visited all the principal chrysanthemum growers in France and the main carnation growers in the States. Within England he won over 250 gold medals, and numerous diplomas, at the RHS, NCS and other shows. He exhibited at the major shows in France, Germany, Austria (14 days delivery), Italy, America – his largest gold medal came from New York – and even Melbourne, Australia, the plants being kept as fresh as possible for the sea journey by being packed in ice! In 1912 he developed "The Queen Mary" chrysanthemum (with specimens donated to the British Queen), though the yellow "Daily Mail" the following year proved more popular. A generation of horticultural enthusiasts held the provenance Wells (Merstham) Ltd. in high esteem. Mr. Wells lived on Battlebridge Lane, in what is now called Shrewsbury House opposite Devon Road, and built a couple of houses next to it for his two sons. With both of them involved in the First World War, he was conscious of the strain on other local families who had menfolk in khaki and gave discreet support to a number of families in the parish. He died early in 1916 and one of his sons shortly afterwards. It was left to the other son, H. Wells, to carry on the business. Mr. H. Wells' son, Ben, took over from his father in the mid 1920s and, with Dr. Weir, produced the Erodium plant called "Merstham Beauty" (reimported to the village only recently by the Taylers). Ben moved the nursery to former Gatton glebe land in 1934 and so it continued, despite extensive bomb damage on 16th April 1941, very much part of the landscape and for the recreational use of the villagers, until 1975, when the then owner, Mr. Hancock, sold it. It was a surprise to find the land being then developed, despite Green Belt restrictions, and the current stark buildings erected, though with a service road suitably named Wells Way.

A much more attractive piece of period architecture is Darby House, on Bletchingley Road. This was built opposite the Pelly's former residence just before the Green Belt restrictions were enacted, for Nutting & Sons Ltd., the seed & bulb merchants, who used it as a packaging and distribution centre for several decades. At present it is used by the School Government Publishing Company Ltd. to produce its annual reference book of all state-run schools.

Apart from Wells Nurseries, horticultural expertise could be found in Sir Jeremiah Colman's Gatton gardens across the A23 (where he specialised in orchids), and the numerous gardeners employed by the gentlemen who had moved into Rockshaw Road. The local Horticultural Society was started in South Merstham, nurtured by such sponsors as Mr. Nicol and Mr. Craker, who had been head gardener at Doods, but soon reaching out to all parts of the village. From an early stage, it was a highly competitive organisation of a very high standard, boasting trophies that would rival the mess silver of many an ancient regiment! Its Treasurer for over 30 years, from about 1926, was P.M. (Percy Morgan) Bennett of 86 Nutfield Road. Although the Merstham Horticultural Society had succeeded in unifying "Old" and "South" Merstham, the arrival of the Estate in 1952 was not viewed as an immediate extension of its membership. Accordingly Mr. "J." **Joiner**, who had recently retired to Bletchingley Road from Queen Elizabeth's School, Leatherhead, got together similar enthusiasts, such as Bill Prevett, and set up the "New Merstham Gardening Society" in Malmestone Avenue. In due course it merged with the Merstham Horticultural Society, a fair symbol of the breakdown of divisions between the two communities. Mr. Joiner was a caring, unselfish person, very supportive of Church social events. He died in 1993, otherwise remembered for his model railway, which he donated to St. Nicholas' School when it moved into Taynton Drive from Redhill.

Landed gentry

A number of the other local pre-war gentry can be found under other chapter headings, so that this section is not intended to denote any form of superiority. It is impossible to try and impose a simple pattern to the shifting influences on the Merstham community: certain families, generally of very different pursuits, were prominent in the community for varied periods. Beyond that, one would be implying an unchanging range and depth of society's interests, and a degree of stamina in individuals, that cannot fit reality.

The **Jolliffe** family had owned Merstham since 1788, a grandson of that purchaser being created Lord Hylton in 1866. The story of the family has been retold in many a local history[25]. At the turn of the century, the 3rd Lord Hylton was living in Ammerdown, SW of Bath, and his Merstham estates were let off to a variety of folk. The family's formal connections with St. Katharine's, and the local Masonic Lodge, lapsed when they became Catholic, though they kept a keen interest in their farms and farmers (and, indeed, the Cricket Club) throughout the period, this interest diminishing in proportion to the reduction in their estates. For, since Merstham House was pulled down in 1950s, portions of the estate have been gradually sold off, so that there are only pockets of land still in the family's control. The Jolliffes have been occasional visitors in the period covered by this composition, but such is their involvement that only a handful of residents, such as Mr. Maurice Stradling of Home Farm, would recognise the present Lord Hylton.

A property that was never part of the Jolliffe estates was a small bit of farmland next to Warwick Wold, that was acquired by Percy Leonard **Pelly** in the mid 19th Century, who duly built Oakley Manor in the style of the period, with an approach road that is now Radstock Way. The family was a junior line of one of the directors of the ancient Hudsons Bay Company. Of the Pelly's five children, the eldest, Percy John Pelly, had built Coppice Lea following his marriage in 1879 to Florence Butler from Chipstead and lived there for the early part of this century. His father, P. L. Pelly JP, had died in 1892, so that, at the

---

[25] The Joliffes were part of Lord Derby's administration, but their period in office was too limited to be able to make much of it (q.v. Hunter's *Gentlemen of Merstham and Gatton*) so that the Radstock estates provided the family with more country pursuits at a time when proximity to London was no longer important to them.

beginning of this century, Oakley was occupied by his mother, Eliza, and possibly his sister, Mabel (Ada and Beatrice had got married in 1890, and his brother, Leonard, died in Essex in 1913). Just as one Mrs. Pelly had been a benefactor to St. Katharine's where her husband had been churchwarden, so the next Mrs. Pelly, as one might also expect of the largest landowner in the new parish, was one of the main benefactors of All Saints. P. J. Pelly had two unmarried daughters, Florence and Doris, so that there were any number of Mrs. and Miss Pellys doing good works in the parish, though the convention of not stating the ladies' initials makes it impossible to be sure which was which. Certainly his mother was still at Oakley in her 90s when P. J. Pelly sold Coppice Lea to the Stephens and moved to Gloucestershire. A Miss Pelly lived at Mead Cottage in Quality Street for a time thereafter. Following the death of Mrs. Pelly in 1924, Oakley was bought by Mr. and Mrs. A. Downs. They had four daughters, Mavis, Sheila, Sybil (who joined All Saints' PC) and Betty, which would have brought the house alive again. After the war, there was little private demand for big houses but those responsible for the Merstham Youth Centre at Broadmead, by the station, were delighted to get Oakley as its better positioned successor site in 1953.

The **Jarchow** family, consisting of Frederick and Anne and their three children, were also in Merstham before the end of the last century. Frederick Jarchow is listed in 1887 as "overseer" at The Villa in Merstham and may well have been Lord Oxenbridge's agent for Gatton, in the way that Harrie Stacey was for the Jolliffe's. The post would have been short-lived as Gatton was sold to Jeremiah Colman the following year. But the Jarchows appear to have had independent means (believed to be inherited from a hatter's business). In 1912 the Jarchows bought the Barn House in Quality Street from Paxton Watson and two of their children became closely involved with the local community. When Mrs. Jarchow was widowed, she moved to "Thirle" at Gatton Point, where she resolutely failed to move with the times, being always dressed in voluminous black and with her hair done on top of her head in a style associated with Queen Mary, George V's consort. One son, Carl, was a prep. school master elsewhere than Merstham. The other two, (Ann) Ulricha and Chris, never married but were very much part of the Merstham community.

Ulricha had joined Maud Roffey and Lottie Stephens in setting up the Merstham Nursing Association, she and Maud

serving with the VAD in the First World War. She was swept up in the war-time enthusiasm for the Women's Institute, becoming the secretary to Merstham's one, from when it was formed in May 1919 through to 1925, by which time there had been four different Presidents. Ulricha was herself its president for 1930. She and her brother were involved in the foundation of the Merstham Operatic and Dramatic Society, the operatic section of which had a brief if dazzling existence, lapsing when no one was found willing to take over responsibility for it. Her musical talent was then restricted to being organist at St. Joseph's, Redhill. She was involved with the Girl Guide movement, the Red Cross and, notably, St John's Ambulance Brigade in which she held the rank of Corps Superintendent. Had women then had the sort of career opportunities that they now take for granted, it would be fascinating to have seen what such talented girls as Miss Jarchow, Miss Roffey and Mrs. Stephens would have done. As it happens, Ulricha is best remembered for her excellent needlework and weaving. Like Maud Roffey, she had become a Catholic and had a Latin funeral following her death in 1952, attended by Rev. Joseph Poole among others. In a spirit of cooperation that was rare for the period, her body was taken from St. Joseph's to be interred in St. Katharine's graveyard, the service being attended by the cream of Merstham society as well as the appropriate representatives of the national bodies that she served.

Chris Jarchow, on the other hand, took an active interest in politics, chairing the local Conservative Association and serving on the Merstham Parish Council until it was abolished in 1933. Several were involved but it seems to have been mainly through his efforts that Quality Street got its name officially, the street sign being funded by a local whip-round. He was "one of Merstham's most prominent residents for many years" whose outstanding characteristic was his sincerity of purpose. He was president of the Village Club, with a keen interest in its snooker championships, Treasurer of St. Katharine's PC and an active supporter of the Cricket Club, for whose fetes he lent Barn House's garden. As already mentioned, he and his sister were involved in the foundation of the Merstham Operatic and Dramatic Society (president: Mme Geraldine Ulmar), the earliest known production of which was Gilbert & Sullivan's *HMS Pinafore* in February 1930. Chris was both its secretary and

Merstham House and Gatton Bottom in 1920s

treasurer. Before the year was over, however, the society had split into the Merstham & District Operatic Society run by Chris, and the Merstham Amateur Dramatic Society, run by George Harris. Chris Jarchow conceived the idea of a performance of *A Midsummer's Night's Dream* in the grounds of Merstham House for the 1935 Jubilee, ably produced by Miss Gwen Lally. He could not manage both that and the Operatic Society, so he tried unsuccessfully to find someone willing to take it over. Four years later the Dramatic Society also lapsed through lack of a volunteer to organise it. At the beginning of the Second World War, Chris Jarchow gave over the Barn House to the Weirs and bought Old Tye Place[26], London Road South, in which to live more modestly. He never lived to see MADS resurrected as he died, aged 64, in 1941.

Merstham was also to be graced with a royal presence. **Princess Arthur of Connaught** (the Duchess of Fife in her own right) had made a formal visit to Redhill and Reigate in June 1918, and must have been suitably impressed: In 1926 she had a house built for her by Nutfield Marsh, but never occupied it. She sold it (later Lancelyn country club) within a year and looked for an alternative: She was taken by Bert Whitaker in a model T Ford hire car to see a couple of sites, one on Shepherds Hill and another on Harps Oak Lane. The latter was chosen, and Whitakers set to work to build Merstham Lodge. Miss Auton recalls how, in 1928, she saw the arrival of a couple of furniture wagons drawn by black horses struggling up the steep incline to unload at the Lodge.[27] How much Her Highness actually used it, is anyone's guess. She was widowed in 1938, but remained the listed owner into the Second World War (when her son died). The property then belonged to Col. John Goad, who was active in the administration of the Boys Brigade, in the '50s, and is currently the home of an accountant, Graham Williams, who is also the present chairman of the Hawthorns board of governors.

[26] Previously a Tea Lounge run by Mrs. Colclough, whose husband was in the pottery trade.
[27] As recounted to Guy Bingham for his column in the County Post, 1977.

Alexandra, Princess Arthur of Connaught

Lawyers and criminals

Most criminal justice is dispensed by unpaid Justices of the Peace who, until recently, were invited to take on such a responsibility. A number of Merstham people mentioned elsewhere held this position, such as Harrie Stacey, John Topham Richardson and Mrs. Ruth Weir in the first half of the century. For a while Mrs. Weir was the only JP from Merstham but, in line with the deliberate move to make the bench more representative of the community, there have been several more since:

Year appointed	Name	Address
1958	Geoffrey Kirk	19, Bolsover Grove
1959	George Searle	27, Orpin Road
	Eileen Whitaker	Downholme, Station Approach
1966	Tim Alleyn	Wisteria Cottage, Quality Street
1966	Jim Danckwerts	Orchard House, Gatton Bottom
1970	Bob Leader	81 Taynton Drive
1972	Joyce Crosfield	Beech Road, Shepherds Hill
1976	Dinkie Leonard	Harps Oak Lane
1978	Bruce Carden	Radstock Way (moved away 1989)
1984	Jean Pearce	School Hill (moved away 1995)
1988	David Jenkins	Laxton Gardens
1988	Carette Pullinger	Mill House, Rockshaw Road (moved away 1994)
1989	Paul Ryder	Bushetts Grove
1998	Ruth Hunter	The Corner House, Church Hill

These are all lay magistrates; metropolitan areas such as London employ stipendiary magistrates, who are professional, paid lawyers. One such was Sybil **Campbell**, of Warwick Wold, who was the first female stipendiary magistrate. She was appointed in about 1946 by Tower Hamlets borough, in which capacity she dealt with those from London's docklands. In the civil commotion there in 1949 she tended to stress the deterrent element in her sentencing policy which gave her a reputation for being harsh, certainly by today's standards.

Of the lay magistrates from Merstham, Geoffrey **Kirk** was a well-liked, ex-Naval gentleman who had worked on the public relations side of the Coal Board, retiring with an OBE for his work at that high profile position only two years after he went on the bench. Those familiar with the politics of the period will understand the difficulty of a job that required dealing with Jo Gormley and Arthur Scargill, however much he himself was a committed member of the Labour Party, working closely with Bob Leader, Bert Monger and Arthur Ball on local matters. His professional tact and understanding were well appreciated in his dealings with the local community issues. He was an avid cricket enthusiast, supporting Derbyshire, the county of his birth, in the summer. In the winter his interest in football would thus be Chesterfield! As a result of several holidays on the Isle of Skye, he bought an intended retirement cottage there, but unfortunately he and a colleague drowned in a boating accident off that island in 1985. Both George Searle and Tim Alleyn became magistrates as a result of having been mayor.

Jim **Danckwerts** was brought up in the law, being the only son of Rt. Hon. Lord Justice Danckwerts, though he himself, on being demobbed from the wartime RAF, went into advertising, coming to live first in Bolsover Grove, then at Orchard House in Gatton Bottom, newly built out of the Rectory's former orchard[28]. A necessary change of career was matched with a move to Rockshaw Road. He was another founder/member of The Merstham Society, being its first chairman in 1960 (his father addressed the Merstham Society in 1963), vice president in 1973 and president from 1981 until his death in 1998. Bob **Leader** was one of those magistrates who resigned over the issue of no discretion for magistrates in the prosecution of Poll Tax defaulters in 1990. Joyce **Crosfield** and her husband have been on Beech Road, off Shepherds Hill, since 1958. He was one of those very senior civil servants, in the Treasury during the period of predominantly Labour Government, retiring in 1978, just before the "Winter of Discontent" that brought down the government. Mrs. Crosfield herself is due to retire after nearly 30 years as a magistrate, just before the millennium. Jean Pearch was already a much respected magistrate for the Croydon area when she moved to School Hill, an appropriate address for a music teacher. She attracted some publicity just after she sold her Merstham home for giving Eric Cantona, a star member of the Manchester United football team, a custodial sentence for his attack on a Crystal Palace fan in 1995.

---

[28] Orchard House then became home to the O'Driscoll family – Pat O'Driscoll was a qualified doctor *and* dentist – and was sold to the Diocese in 1986 when the former Rectory was put on the market. Orchard House was renamed the Rectory, as it is the present home for the rector of Merstham and Gatton.

As mentioned in the press at the time, she was known to be fair rather than tough. Carette Pullinger and Dinkie Leonard were both judges' wives. Mrs. Pullinger lived with her husband, John Pullinger at the Mill House on Rockshaw Road, until she moved to Reigate in 1994. Lady Leonard died tragically in 1996 shortly after being hit by rock fragments after a lightening strike in Cyprus. She was much mourned by those in Merstham who knew her.

Her husband, Sir (Hamilton) John **Leonard** always intended to be a barrister, with even his military service in the Guards being mainly spent with a Court-Martial unit in post-war Germany. It was through this that he met his future wife, being married at 22 in 1948. Early years as a barrister are financially more difficult than most people realise, and it was through a lot of hard work that he earned the position of first, junior prosecuting counsel, then Common Sergeant (full-time judge), at The Old Bailey. About this time (mid 1960s) he and Dinkie bought Field End on Harps Oak Lane from the Lees. He was knighted and appointed a High Court judge, Queens Bench division, in 1981. In 1987 he provoked outrage from the press when he sentenced the perpetrator of the Ealing vicarage rape case to only 5 years in jail, plus 5 for burglary, compared with 14 years for his accomplice's burglary and assault. It is a reflection of the power of the media that he found himself instantly judged by his neighbours and fellow commuters. It is a tribute to him that he took the opportunity of a presentation to the Merstham Society to explain, more fully than the papers had done, all the various aspects of the case and what had led to his judgement. When he retired in 1993, he made a public apology to the victim, thereby regaining in stature more than he had lost.

There are fewer Merstham notables on the other side of the law, but no history of the village would be complete without mentioning the connection of Ronald **Biggs** to the locality. After a spell in prison for petty crime in South London, Ronald "went straight", taking up carpentry and staying with a "pretty tough lady" at Merstham called Ivy, who was a friend of Bruce Reynolds, a fellow jailbird. Once he found his feet, he moved to Redhill, doing a number of small refurbishment jobs locally, including Merstham and, in 1960, he married the daughter of the headmaster of Reigate Parish School, who was already expecting their first child. It was the arrival of a second child, however, that made Ron feel financially insecure and thus vulnerable to the suggestions of Bruce Reynolds who made him a partner in the Great Train Robbery of August 1963. He was in the middle of decorating Wellhead, the Batchelors' home in Gatton Bottom, just beforehand and told them he would "be away for a week or two". There had not been such a high value crime for generations and the way it was done, and the subsequent capture, and escape, of Ron Biggs are all a matter of popular history. Less well known, however, is the suicide of his father-in-law and the emigration of his wife to the comparative anonymity of Australia.

There will have been other local criminals, but none of Ron Biggs' fame. The nearest the locality has produced since (and it is a tribute to the village that it is not a den of villains) was the gentleman who took over Boars Green Farm on Harps Oak Lane in the 1980s. Stephen **Prior** was featured in a investigative programme on the radio, such was the public interest in his career. However, it has proved impossible for the author to separate fact from fiction with regard to his past, and even Stephen's limp has been ascribed to be the result of action taken by a jealous husband! Certainly he had a natural charm but it failed to sway the borough officials with whom he clashed swords on a number of occasions as he tried various developments on his estate. It has been some years since he left Merstham but his former neighbours still refer to him with cautious respect.

Flour bomb, Portland Drive 1953

Literary and artistic characters

"Imagine a person, tall, lean and feline, high shouldered with a brow like Shakespeare, and a face like Satan, a close-shaven skull and long magnetic eyes of the true cat-green. Imagine that awful being and you have a mental picture of Dr. Fu Manchu, the yellow peril incarnate in one man." British crime writers have created some memorable heroes, such as Sherlock Holmes, Lord Peter Wimsey, Fr. Brown and Hercule Poirot, but no villain had so great a following as Fu Manchu did. His popularity was ascribed partly to the successful contrast of everyday tools of the criminal trade employed against a decidedly exotic background, and partly to the character of the arch-villain himself, who conducted himself with impeccable integrity and superior intellect, being only foiled by either chance or betrayal, usually by a female accomplice falling in love with his pursuer. This was the creation of Sax Rohmer, one-time resident of Merstham. Sax Rohmer was actually the nom de plume adopted by one Arthur Henry Sarsfield Ward. He was a 17 year old lad from Birmingham at the turn of the century and soon employed as a reporter to cover the underworld goings-on in the notorious Limehouse area of London's East End. He was only 29 when he created Fu Manchu and he went on to produce a host of stories based on this character (and a few others), being published from 1913 through to his death in 1959, with only the Second World War as an interval. In the 1920's he lived in Hazelton, a house that used to be on Battlebridge Lane by the corner with Devon Road. Such was the increasing popularity of his books, however, that he moved from there to join the British community on the Atlantic island of Madeira and would appear to have stayed there throughout the peak of his character's popularity during the 1930s. Appropriately enough, his only Club membership, in an age when any gentleman had to belong to at least one London Club, was the Eccentric Club.

Young Sax Rohmer was not the only journalist to pass through Merstham. The international news agency, Reuters, maintained a transit house at Gatton Point and one of their bright young reporters, Doon **Campbell**, stayed there a couple of times. On the first occasion, he had completed a spell as war correspondent having been the first (and, at 25, one of the youngest) such to land on the Normandy beaches on D-Day, 6

June 1944, with Lovat's Commandos, from which he followed the Allied advance to the Rhine and beyond. He knew the reality of the battles and the horror of Belsen concentration camp first hand. On the second occasion, in 1948, he had just completed a spell covering the Palestine Mediation Mission, having previously been closely involved with the events leading up to, and following, Indian Partition and Gandhi's assassination. To quote Doon: "The house at that time had four or five male guests and to help balance the party, Harold Carter invited two young ladies he knew from amateur dramatic occasions at Merstham". One of them was Mary Toms and she and Doon were engaged before the end of the year. They were married in June 1949 at St. Katharine's and moved to Vanves, a village in a similar relationship to Paris as Merstham is to London. Here Doon became Reuter's Paris News Editor (and where one of the staff, Freddy Forsyth, was later to write his *Day of the Jackal*), but there was no real change to his itinerant lifestyle until he was promoted to become one of Reuters' three newly-created Deputy General Managers in 1963. He was the last to retire, a decade later, and then worked for United Newspapers and the Commonwealth Press Union, being awarded his OBE in 1984. Being based on Rockshaw Road, Doon was able to share his varied and vivid experiences with members of The Merstham Society on three or four separate occasions between 1962 and 1994. They had just moved from Rockshaw Road to Church Hill when Mary died in 1995. Doon has always had one arm, but it never held him back – and certainly never stopped him typing or taking shorthand – and he describes his career as foreign correspondent as being, above all, fun.

Another post war arrival was Jack **Hillier**, brought up in Redhill but who had spent much of the war in RAF Signals in the Middle East. In 1947 he moved with his wife and two young children into 173 Albury Road from which he commuted to his work for an insurance company in London – not the most exciting occupation for a 35 year old who otherwise enjoyed wood engraving and painting[29]. Stimulated by a set of Japanese prints he found in a London book market, he began to learn all he could about the genre. In 1954, he published *Masters of the Japanese Colour Print* and then did monographs on Hokusai and Utamaro, as a result of which he was invited by Sotheby's to

---

[29] His first book was *Old Surrey Watermills* (1951) with his own illustrations

become consultant expert on Japanese prints, paintings and books. Jack set about becoming proficient in Japanese, often studying on the Merstham train to and from work. In due course the quality of the work he did in collecting and writing about Japanese illustrated books was rewarded, in 1992, with the highest class of the Order of the Rising Sun from the Japanese government. He had moved to Redhill in 1958 but his son, Bevis Hillier, himself a writer on fine arts, has fond memories of growing up in South Merstham, which he wrote up for the *Country Living* magazine in 1994. Bevis lists among his recreations "awarding marks out of ten for suburban front gardens".

Another person captivated by the Orient is the naturalist, Bill **Smythies**. He was working in Rangoon in the 1930s and produced the first definitive book on *The Birds of Burma* in 1940. When the Japanese invaded some months later, they had the unsold copies shipped back to their Emperor where they fell victim to the destructive bombing that brought an end to the war with Japan. There have been a couple of editions of the book since, but a 1940 original is now quite a collectors' item. Mr. Smythies went on to become an expert on the jungles (and birds) of Borneo, before coming to Merstham. Together with his wife, who was a botanical illustrator, they have been involved in several publications since. Few who saw the modest couple on their regular walks from their home at the top of Church Hill, would have been aware of their encyclopedic knowledge of botanical matters.

There is a large number of people who enjoy collecting things and, in the affluence of post-war South East England, they have been able to indulge their hobbies. The one person who must be mentioned in the context of Merstham is Peter **White,** who used to do research work in the BBC. He has collected the most comprehensive collection of postcards of Merstham which gives a useful glimpse of the village's structures in the last 110 years.

Another talented family that moved into Merstham after the last world war was the Wheelers. Charles **Wheeler** was a sculptor and painter who spent most of his life based in Chelsea and South Kensington. He was best known for his sculptures: the Indian Army war memorial at Neuve Chapelle, the Jellicoe bust and fountain in Trafalgar Square, the stone statue of Charles Montague for the Bank of England and a bronze of Yehudi Menuhin, for example. He was 57 and had just finished

7 years as a Trustee of the Tate Gallery when he bought Weavers in Warwick Wold as the family's country retreat. While he was here, he became president of the Royal Academy (1956 – 1966) and was duly knighted in 1958[30]. He gave a talk on the Fine Arts to the Merstham Society in 1965. His wife Muriel was a fellow sculptor and painter, exhibiting, with her husband, at the Royal Academy for most years in the two decades that they were associated with Merstham. She was a member of the Society of Women Artists, as was her daughter, Carol Wheeler, who exhibited a number of oil paintings from 1950 to 1962. The Wheelers kept a London address but cemented their ties with Merstham when they bought North Cottage in Quality Street in the mid '60s. Sir Charles Wheeler did a number of paintings of the Surrey Hills around Merstham, the last one in 1974 just before his death, being entitled *Before the Motorway*.

In 1953 a retired 69-year-old solicitor was visiting cousins at Rockshaw House and noticed The Georgian House on Rockshaw Road was up for sale. It was ideal for his collection of paintings, and Kerrison and Evelyn **Preston** duly moved in with those of their children who remained unmarried (they had lost one of their sons at Tobruk in 1942). Mr. Preston had an interest in Romanticism, as evidenced by his book *Blake and Rosetti*. He had been executor of the estate of W. Graham Robertson who had a vast collection of William Blake effects, and was responsible not only for its auction, but also for the donation of several pieces to British galleries, and of the Blake Library to Westminster City. His wife, who had been a staunch supporter of Merstham's church and W.I., died the year after this last donation, in 1968. From then until his own death in 1974, Mr. Preston's recreations were listed as "books, pictures and grandchildren". Others would remember him for the small trilby perched on top of his head.

It may seem that the work of Merstham's cultured families appealed to a select few, but there were also Merstham writers who catered for a wider audience. One need only mention Andrew and Penny **Stanway** of Shepherds Hill, who were both best sellers in their own right. Dr. Penny Stanway was best known for her *"Breast is Best"* for mothers of the '80s; while Andrew wrote a number of books aimed at restoring sexual consideration in marriages. Merstham has never been out of tune with the national *zeitgeist*.

---

[30] Sir Charles Wheeler's autobiography, *"High Relief"*, was published in 1968.

Medical practitioners

The village's first local doctor was Dr. Henry **Crickett** who was a medical officer with the London, Brighton & South Coast Railway and settled in Merstham in the 1890s, about the same time that South Merstham was being developed beside the new "quarry line" of the railway. His practice in the High Street (South Lodge, a late Georgian double fronted building) grew fast, as the village population doubled to some 2,000 people within that decade. Very late on the night of Sunday 24th September 1905 he was summoned by the police to examine the smashed body of a young lady of about 21 years old, which had been found in Merstham Tunnel. It was assumed that she had committed suicide but Dr. Crickett found sufficient evidence, including a silken gag in her mouth, to call it murder. He thought she must have come out of the carriage "full stretch", hands and feet sliding helplessly on the wall of the tunnel. After striking the wall, Dr. Crickett said, she must have rebounded and fallen under the wheels of the train and so received her many injuries. Although the later inquest concluded there was insufficient evidence to tell whether she fell or was thrown to her death, the testimony of a signalman at Purley Oaks, who saw a man and woman struggling in a carriage on the down train at about the right time that night, lent credence to Dr. Crickett's opinion. The Merstham Tunnel Mystery, as it became known, was never solved. Dr. Crickett was also, as his name suggests, a cricketer, becoming captain of Merstham's Cricket Club in 1901.

Dr Crickett had a Scottish stepson, Walter **Weir**, who was also a doctor and joined the practice in 1907. He was as keen a cricketer as his stepfather, playing against the legendary W.G. Grace at Crystal Palace in 1908. Three years later he married Ruth Bell, whom he had met while doing a locum in the Midlands, and duly purchased his stepfather's practice. A year later, their first child, Joy, was born. With the start of the First World War, Dr. Weir took on the additional duties of medical officer to the local Voluntary Aid Detachment for repatriated wounded which had been set up in Chaldon Rise, towards the end of Rockshaw Road. After the birth of their son, Christopher, in 1916, Dr. Weir joined the RAMC and was shipped off to Mesopotamia, returning to South Lodge (and the 'flu epidemic) in 1920. He joined Merstham's branch of the newly founded British Legion, and had been elected President by 1927. He was very much part of the Legion's social scene and would often be found in the Albury Road club house, quaffing an evening pint after a day's work. By then the Weirs had moved to The Bell House in London Road South, leaving South Lodge to Walter Bell of Langley & Bell, wine merchants – the property was demolished in the mid '30s. The traffic on the A23 was already dangerous then: In 1929 Dr. Weir was hit by a car and carried to the nearest house, which had a doctor's plate on the door – his own, much to the shock of his daughter, Joy, who was the one to answer the door! She herself contracted and died of diphtheria before the end of the year, a tragic blow that hit the village hard, especially as it turned out that another local teenage girl, Diana Topham Richardson, had died in a Sussex hospital the same day. Dr. Weir was still suffering from his accident to the extent that, some five years later, he had to have his leg amputated, making him a noticeable figure on his rounds. Ruth too was very much part of the community, being president of the W.I. both from 1922-25 and from 1931-33. She was also a local magistrate, for some time the only one from Merstham. A frequent visitor was her brother, R. W. Bell, who wrote stories under the pen-name of Keble Howard and was editor of a boys paper called "Captain". With the advent of the Second World War, the Weir's son, Christopher, joined the Cameronians and was with the BEF in the retreat to Dunkirk, acquitting himself sufficiently well to be later awarded the MC. About this time, the Weirs moved to the Barn House in Quality Street (the Jarchow's former home) and ran the practice from there, with a maid and all the personal quirks of a pre-NHS practice. Dr. Weir retired in 1957 and, by the time he died, in 1967, he had been some 60 years in the village.

   The growth of Redhill in the inter war period had made it logical for Dr. Weir to combine his practice with some colleagues covering that parish (their history is told in a booklet on the Reigate borough doctors) and in 1942 the partnership brought in Dr. E. John **Tucker** to help cover the Merstham area. John had been unable to do military service due to a disease of the tibia. He moved into Oakhurst, 97 Nutfield Road (another Paxton Watson building), so that he is best remembered by residents of South Merstham, leaving Walter Weir with St. Katharine's parishioners. At this time the practice was conducted from The Barn House and Oakhurst, with a district nurse, Mrs. Frances **Augarde**, who had been South

Merstham's medical officer before the war, and who lived at 2 Dean's Road. Then she had covered her parish by bicycle; postwar she became equally well known for her tiny vehicle and her constant canine companions, an unusual combination of large and small, though there is some debate whether she bred Great Danes or Boxers.

The end of the Second World War was duly celebrated with a programme of events organised by the Merstham Peace Celebrations Committee which was drawn from all parts of the village, and chaired by Dr. Tucker. With the introduction of the National Health in 1948, everyone had a doctor, and the creation of the LCC estate doubled the number of patients in Merstham, effectively moving the weight of this partnership from Redhill to Merstham. Dr. Tucker's cousin, Dr. Robert **Tayler**, was invited to join the practice in 1951 and moved into Oakhurst with his wife and the first two of their children, Dr Tucker moving to Wood Cottage in Warwick Wold with his four children. Each doctor had about 3,500 patients and was on call 24 hours a day, 7 days a week. Before automated connections, Gladys Orange[31], the switchboard operator at Merstham's telephone exchange in Station Road, with her distinctive voice, was effectively an extension of the practice. Dr. Roger **Redd** joined a couple of years later, and Dr. Kenneth **Trigg** (of Middle Fell in Rockshaw Road; his wife was Dr. Jordan who was featured in an article about peripatetic care) in 1960. In 1954, Ruth Weir bought Ashdown House in Bletchingley Road to act as a proper practice building, and Phyllis **Watts** succeeded nurse Augarde, living at 1 Malmstone Avenue. Nurse Watts was a midwife who had worked in the West Indies prior to coming to Merstham. She then married the headmaster of St. Joseph's and thus became known as nurse **Sheenan**. Between them these two nurses were responsible, with the doctors, for bringing nearly all of this generation of Merstham children into the world. The current Moat House health centre was set up when Government funding became available in 1972. It was a curious coincidence that two of the doctors had their homes compulsorily purchased by that same Government in 1972-74, Wood Cottage falling to the M23, Oakhurst for the Chalkmead institution. Robert Tayler moved to Merlebank, Church Hill. John Tucker moved up to Pilgrim's Hill, taking over the

---

[31] Miss Orange lived at "Dalveen" on the corner of Shepherds Hill and Beech Road, for over 60 years. She died in 1998, aged 95, in Coppice Lea nursing home.

Lambert's house. He had been on the Board of the Hawthorns and, when its finances looked precarious in 1978, called on Anthony Stephens for advice. The situation was resolved, but the then chairman died suddenly and Dr. Tucker was reluctantly persuaded to take the Chair. He retired from practice, and the school, moving to the West Country in about 1980, and died shortly afterwards

The main medical establishment in the parish, at least until the reorganisation of boundaries in 1933, was the Surrey County Lunatic Asylum at Netherne. It was one of four late Victorian mental hospitals in the area (Banstead's London, Caterham's Metropolitan, and Coulsdon's London County asylums being the other three), built to a very high standard in 1907-9. 24-year-old Dr. Leonard **Webber** joined the staff of half a dozen doctors in 1910 and, apart from active service in the RAMC during the First World War (in which he was wounded), spent all his career at Netherne. He was its Medical Superintendent from 1934 until his death in 1941. In spite of, or maybe because, he spent his life dealing with the saddest aspects of humanity, he was known to be easily approachable and kind and considerate in manner. A keen sportsman himself, he encouraged others also, so that Merstham Cricket Club included Messrs. Jupp and Grimshaw among their better players, both male nurses at the Netherne. A generation later, the Government in the mid 1990s reversed the approach taken to caring for the mentally afflicted in one purpose-built building with all the benefits of scale associated with such concentrations, and released the patients into the community. In the case of Netherne, a large proportion have returned to this parish, being housed on the estate. The policy has recently been put on hold so that the Netherne site is neither fully utilised nor ripe for development.

There were, of course, other local families involved in medicine. Some were involved with nearby Redhill General hospital, such as nurse Dawes (later Mrs Gwynne), daughter of the long established Dawes of School Hill. Some were more distant, such as Dr. Tom Hills who commuted from his Church Hill House home to his Wimpole Street practice at a time when that Harley Street area of London represented the peak of the profession globally. And there were some in between, such as Dr. Gwen Cole of Merrow, Glebe Road. Of the next generation of physicians, there was one who never saw his 45th birthday: John Hammond, of

Merstham fair, Edwardian period

The 'up platform', Merstham station 1981

82

London Road North, was an anaesthetist at the East Surrey Hospital when he succumbed to a particularly virulent form of cancer in 1995. It was a shocking loss, as he was a kind, patient soul with a good sense of humour and an entertaining gift for music.

On a lighter note, Nutfield Road was enlivened for a while by the Norwegian dentist, Dr. Otto **Nokvam**, who flew the Norwegian flag from the flagpole that he erected in the front garden of no. 35. The traditional fear of a visit to the dentist was dispelled by the attractive young ladies whom he recruited as assistants from Norway, though not always, it seems, bothering to obtain the appropriate work permits. He was similarly lax about obtaining planning permission for a large "sauna" he erected for them in the rear garden. His next brush with the authorities was over his collection of guns, which were duly confiscated. He also set up a first class Norwegian restaurant in Reigate (where Bottoms Up now operates), though this end of the business seems to have been much less profitable in the 1980s than the cheaper end of the business has proved to be more recently. For it is reputed that Dr. Otto went bankrupt and had to be deported back to Norway. A sad end to one who made South Merstham so colourful.

Priests, rectors and vicars

At the beginning of the century, Merstham boasted two parishes, the ancient one of St. Katharine's and the then recently established All Saints for the new development of South Merstham. The Rev. R. **Woodhouse** had been rector of St. Katharine's since 1894 and had been instrumental in setting up first a Mission Room, and then a fully-fledged separate parish in South Merstham. Apart from publishing his *Life of Cardinal Morton*, and *The Poetical Works of James Woodhouse*, he also researched a lot of Merstham's history, which formed the basis of his granddaughter Mary's published work *History of Merstham*. When the new Lord Hylton started developing Church Hill, Mr. Woodhouse did a land swop to enable the Verger's Cottage[32] to be built in 1904. Mr. Woodhouse was already in his 50's at this time. He, and his predecessors, had always sat on the village School Board but it was replaced by the County-run board of managers from 1903 whose views were broader than the emphasis on the 4 "R"s (religion, reading, 'riting & 'rithmatic) of his day. His views were considered "folly and unwisdom" and out of touch with the educational needs of 1912[33]. The Woodhouse's only son Courtenay joined the Army and was commissioned in 1911 with the highest marks of his year. After the required year with a home regiment, he went out to join the Indian Army. He saw action against the Turks at the Suez Canal and met his death near Aden in 1916, four of his same-named cousins having already fallen in the first 2 years of the war. He was 25 years old. Of his two sisters, Helen became a devout Sunday School teacher living in The Cottage in Quality Street until her death in 1966 aged 76, and is remembered in the inscription on The Epiphany's foundation stone. Rosamund, who nursed abroad during the first war, where she met her future husband, became well known to the next Merstham generation as cub mistress. The rector was of course heavily involved with the peace and memorial committees at the end of "the war to end all wars", made personally poignant by the loss of his own heir. He retired to Reigate in 1921, dying a year later. When St. Katharine's churchyard was extended with the

[32] This was occupied by Herbert Glassup who served as verger to several rectors until his death in 1950, and is best remembered as St. Katharine's choirmaster.
[33] Quoted in J. Neil's "*The History of Merstham School*"

purchase of the land on the East side of the A23, its lychgate was dedicated to the Woodhouse family.

Coincidentally, South Merstham's vicar died within months of Mr. Woodhouse. The first vicar of All Saints, Mr. Brocklehurst, had been Mr. Woodhouse's curate and did not stay long. So the incumbent from 1900 was Rev. William **London** whose wife immediately founded a local branch of the Mothers' Union. She went on to be one of the founding members of Merstham's W.I., being elected its first President in 1919.

Another cleric of this generation was Rev. A. G. **Rogers**, rector of St. Andrew's, Gatton. He had an unconventional background for a clergyman, being educated in Coblenz in the Rhineland before going to Durham University. He then travelled extensively, living in Buenos Aires, Jamaica, Rio, Malta and Gibraltar, getting married in the meantime. His wife, Mabel, would have been delighted when, at 34, he took Holy Orders in suburban Kent. After the minimum five years as curate of Kingsdown, he was appointed rector to Colman's Gatton living in 1894. It was after his two sons had joined the forces in 1912, that he moved from the Towers, an ornate building overlooking Gatton Bottom, to a house on Rockshaw Road that he renamed Kingsdown. The Gatton Rectory was thus in Merstham some decades before the parishes were merged, which happened on his retirement, at 80, in 1937, after 43 years as rector of Gatton. Mr. Rogers was, unusually, chaplain to both Surrey (1922) and Sussex (1927) Sheriffs. His eldest son, Maj. Wilfred F. Rogers DSO, was killed in command of his artillery battery in the battle of Arras in 1917 aged 26. The younger son, Philip, survived, after serving in the Navy under Lord Jellicoe, to bring up his own family, while their sister also married and lived at nearby Buckland. When Mrs Rogers was widowed in 1946, she stayed on in Merstham until her own death in 1954, aged 94.

As can be seen from the list, there were a number of elderly rectors and vicars who passed through Merstham thereafter. In 1931 the new rector of St. Katharine's, A. E. **Wilkinson** MC, was 49 years old and so would have been a breath of fresh air to the younger parishioners. He had earned his MC while serving as a chaplain in the First World War, and was vicar of St. James' Croydon between then and taking on St. Katharine's. He enjoyed both cricket and golf, and took a keen interest in Merstham School, coaching the boys in football, as well as encouraging them to join the choir and come to Sunday School. Within six years he added Gatton to his responsibility. In 1941, in the middle of the Second World War, he was again recalled to the Forces and was Chaplain General to the Forces in Northern Ireland. He returned to the parish for the last few years of his ministry, dying in office in 1949.

In South Merstham, Rev. Henry Grant **Baker** was in his 80s for the most tragic time in its history: Merstham had suffered limited damage through the early stages of the Battle of Britain and the Blitz but, on 19th April 1941, the railway was straddled by a couple of parachuted landmines. The one in Wells Nursery failed to explode, but the other one exploded by All Saints church, killing 9 people and injuring several others who were mostly standing by the bus stop[34], the highest local casualty incident of the war. Mary Clark has never forgotten the experience of being bowled over by the blast, which also rendered her temporarily deaf. There was nearly another victim: Ron Shaw, in his capacity as ARP warden, was doing a last check for casualties in the pitch dark and fell into the water-filled crater. Not being able to swim, it was fortunate that a colleague was still with him to pull him out. It was one of Merstham's war-time visitors who initiated the erection of a temporary church, Rev. George **Wolfendale**. It seems we see the brightest stars for the briefest intervals: Mr. Wolfendale had been English born and bred (educated at Oundle), served as a teenager in the Great War, was a stowaway to Canada where he found his vocation in the Anglican ministry, volunteering for missionary work in the Canadian North West. With the outbreak of the second war, he enlisted, not as a chaplain because the waiting list was too long, but as a medical orderly. It was in this capacity that Corporal Wolfendale found himself stationed in Merstham at the time of the land mine, and able to take on the vicar's pastoral duties while Mr. Baker was hors du combat. He received his commission into the chaplaincy about a year later, which gave him more influence to argue that replacing the church was "essential war work". In 1943 he was able to set about organising the erection of a replacement timber hall, similar to those he had erected in British Colombia a decade earlier, out of the salvaged remains of All Saints. It was completed within 5 weeks with Canadian labour and Canada

[34] Those killed were the vicar's sister Sarah Baker (90), an ARP warden Anthony Findlay (17), of 104 Nutfield Road, William Corke (16) of 46 Brook Road, William Shepherd (43) of Devon Road, Cecilia and Billy Kemp (42 & 10) of 46 Nutfield Road, Hannah and Brian Trussler (39 & 13) of 4 The Pavement, and Albert Willoughby (64) of 205 Albury Road who died two months later.

Hall remains to this day the best memorial to our transatlantic visitors. Sadly, Capt. Wolfendale was to die of his wounds in Italy in May 1944. Mr. Baker died in office with the end of the war assured. Canada Hall was used for Anglican worship until All Saints was rebuilt in 1952, whereupon it became the community's social centre for a number of organisations.

There had been a Baptist mission chapel in the High Street since 1874 but it had never achieved enough of a following to become independent of its Redhill parent, and was run from there. This ornate little Victorian building became sufficiently dilapidated by 1950 to be declared unsafe. Mr. Houlder bought it and the Baptist community built their present chapel in Weldon Way, it being opened in 1955. In 1958 Rev. Ronald **Ayres** was appointed its first full-time minister and put his church "on the map", so to speak. He was a good friend of Skip Williamson and was one of many who helped make Oakley Youth Centre a success. Sadly, but in line with its diminished congregation, the chapel has had a succession of more part-time pastors and stand-in moderators to handle its small community since 1983.

A Methodist chapel had been built, also in the Victorian Gothic style, at the corner of Nutfield Road and Bourne Road in South Merstham in 1909. However its community members shrank in line with the national decline in Methodism, so that by the 1930s the building had already been turned over to secular use, housing the local borough library. After a brief occupation by a religious sect, it was pulled down in 1977 and three houses built on the site. The library moved first to The Village Hall, and then to its present purpose-built block in Weldon Way. Its future is currently in some doubt.

Britain was still a church-going nation when Merstham's population was increased by the thousands of Londoners who came with the estate. The LCC had earmarked a plot for a separate parish church and it was duly built in 1955, under the aegis of St. Katharine's PC and the Southwark diocese. At the time, recently rebuilt All Saints had a low church reputation fostered by Cyril Brown, so it was decided to introduce a priest-in-charge of a high church persuasion, to provide a balance in the Merstham community at large. Accordingly Rev. Jack **Clark** was introduced and it was his choice that the church be dedicated to The Epiphany, as he had previously operated from The Epiphany church in East Dulwich when his appointed church in that London suburb was bomb damaged. He proved

to be a very popular vicar, providing good local support to growing families in the short time he was here. His successor was of a similar training, being known as *Father* Dudley.

The local Catholics, or Roman Catholics as they were then called, had gone to Redhill for their services, but the sudden increase following the arrival of the Londoners put too much of a strain on St. Joseph's. Accordingly, from All Saints day (1 November) in 1953, Cyril Brown put Canada Hall at the disposal of Merstham's 200-strong Catholic community, pending the building of their own church. To this end, Messrs Jim Hale of 102 Malmestone Avenue, Paddy Doyle of 55 Wood Street, Jack McCarthy of 75 Taynton Drive, Laurie Benson of 22 Mansfield Drive and Ken Longley of Bankside, Bletchingley Road were the principal organisers of the Football Pools fundraising effort, though most of the estate, not only its Catholic element, was involved. Tim Alleyn, the Catholic architect of the Epiphany, was commissioned to design the building, which he did without the same maintenance-heavy flat roofs. Given the necessarily close working relationship between the Anglicans and the Catholics over Canada Hall, it is interesting to note that Cyril Brown's sucessor, Rev. John Stonehouse, had previously been a Catholic priest. When St. Teresa's was built in 1958/9, it was entirely out of working class (to use the classification of the period) money and to this day there are those who say the circle around its steeple crucifix should represent a football! Its first designated parish priest, Fr. Thomas **Sheehy**, was initially lodged at *The Cottage of Content* pub in the High Street through 1958/9, leading almost a mendicant existence, asking his parishioners for an occasional square meal, and sometimes sleeping in the church sacristy to be on call if need arose, until the priest's house was built.

At St. Katharine's, Mr. Wilkinson had been succeeded by Rev. Joseph **Poole**, whose love of music inspired the new generation of parishioners to join the choir. Of his five children, one son, Quentin, became senior chorister at King's, Cambridge which led to him being the youngest person to be featured on the popular radio programme, *Desert Island Discs*. Apart from music, Mr. Poole had an interest in typography. He left Merstham in 1958 to become Precentor of Coventry Cathedral.

Meanwhile, All Saints continued its tradition of elderly vicars, the latest, Justice **Becke**, having been a chartered

All Saints Church after the parachute bomb 1941

accountant in his youth. However, it was he that set up the Wives Group in 1965, a social gathering that lasted 30 years. His wife was a policewoman, and became the Metropolitan Police's first woman superintendent in the mid '60s. Becke was followed by a much younger vicar, Richard **Lewis**, who, together with his wife Jill, reached out to the young families, especially those recently arrived on the new Wates estate. He enjoyed music and was not above taking his clarinet into the pulpit. He succeeded in rejuvenating the parish and went on to achieve the same turn-around in a couple of other parishes before being promoted to Dean of Wells in 1990 (he was also chaplain of Alleyn's, Dulwich from 1979-90). But thereafter, his successor from 1972, along with his fellow churchmen in the area (including the Catholic priests, after the traumatic change brought about by the Second Vatican Council of 1968), presided over a steady decline in numbers, though there has been some reversal of this trend in recent years which bodes better for the millennium.

The acceptance by the Anglican Church of women priests was achieved in 1994 after years of preparation. Both Miss Marian Randall and Christine Millar had become deacons (not "deaconess", to avoid confusion with the Baptist title) in 1987, but it was not until 1989 that Miss Millar took over the long vacant position at the Epiphany (its churchwarden, Les Longshaw, having somehow kept it going in the interval) and it was here she got married, becoming Mrs Wheeler, only moving away at the time of her first child. After another gap, the current vicar, Christine Latham, was appointed on the basis that the NHS Trust provides half her funding, in relation to the number of people in community care now on the estate.

Of course the Christian values are not confined to church attendance. There has been, and continues to be, a large number of people involved in charitable organisations. To pick one example from the many of Merstham's community who have been so involved in such work is not to belittle the others in any way: Jack and Daphne **Gloster-Smith** came to Meadowside in Devon Road just after the Second World War and Daphne was soon involved in doing case-work for the Forces Help Society. She is better remembered, though, for her work in setting up and organising the Redhill & Reigate Citizens Advice Bureau. She started in 1956 in the days before legal advice was part of the offered service and officially retired in 1979, being awarded an MBE for her work in this connection

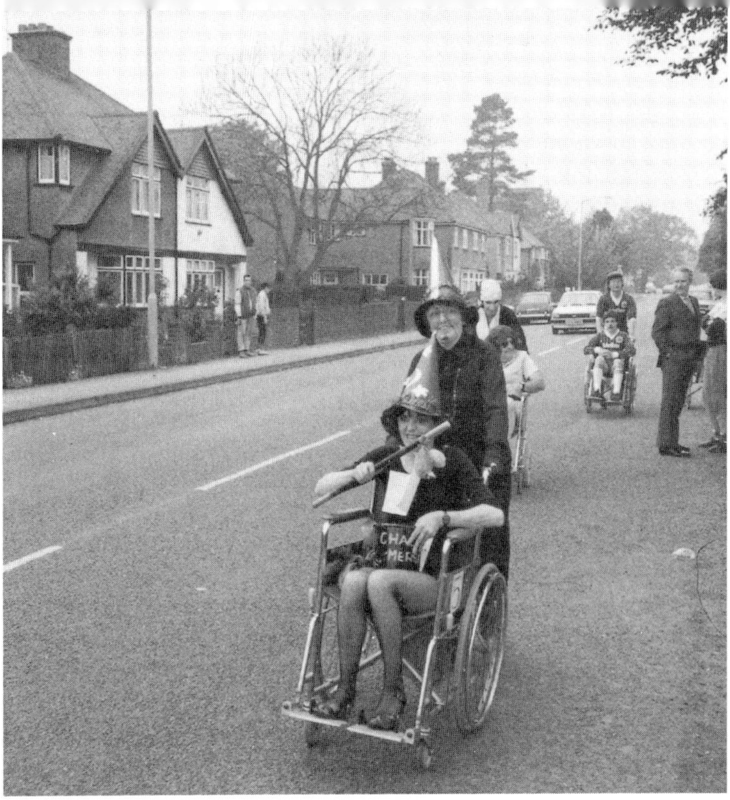

1985 sponsored wheelchair race, Nutfield Road

Quality Street Fair 1980s

in 1982. She was also vice chairman of Surrey County Council's committee for Social Services Citizens Advice for a time. Inevitably her interest in the community extended to other aspects, including the Peace Commemoration Suppers, Netherne Hospital and the Surrey Community Development Trust. She died in 1990, being survived by her husband.

Apart from the obvious dedicated purpose charities such as Help the Aged, Victim Support, Dr. Barnardo's, The Red Cross etc., there is an important charitable side to such social groups as the Masonic Lodge, the Round Table, Rotary, Lions and Soroptomists Clubs which have their local meetings in Reigate and Redhill, and to which any number of Merstham individuals have contributed and continue to contribute their time as much as their donations. Then there is the Merstham Aid Project, which is a similar sort of selfless operation, different more for its local title than for its aims and activities, which mirror those of the other, more internationally recognised, clubs. MAP was founded by Mary and Jack **Hughes** from Sutton Gardens in 1982 following a presentation from an earlier established overseas aid trust. In its effort to raise funds to finance third world projects, it has run the full gambit of social events, sponsored physical exercise (including a 350 mile walk by Jack and a parachute jump by Mary 18 months after her heart attack), plant and jumble sales, while its third world beneficiaries include Eye Camps, Sweet Water projects, and VSO volunteers. Without the support of a national parent body, it nearly foundered when its founders retired from the leadership in 1991, but there has been enough local support to take it on to the next century.

The millennium is a celebration of 2,000 years of Christianity. Those who have served full-time in His ministry in Merstham these last 100 years are thus listed in total:

St. Katharine's rectors

1894	R. I. WOODHOUSE c.1856–1922, 1917 Rural Dean Reigate
1921	Arthur H. R. ROBINSON c.1878–1945 buried in Merstham
1926	Eyre CHATTERTON 1863–195?, 1903–26 Bishop of Nagpur
1931	Agmond E. WILKINSON OBE, MC 1882–1949 from 1937, Gatton included
1949	Joseph W. POOLE 1909–1989, 1958 Precentor of Coventry
1959	John H. BIDDELL 1915–
1966	Philip E. DUVAL MBE b.1918. 1978 Hon. Canon Southwark
1987	Royston J.M. GROSVENOR 1947–
1998	John E. SMITH 1952–

St. Teresa's priests

1955	Thomas SHEEHY
1972	MAXWELL
1975	Michael HILL
1979	H. Benet WOODMAN
1994	Hugh FLOWER

Baptist chapel

1958	Ronald AYRES
1965	John HOPPER
1968–1983	Dennis FLOODGATE

All Saints' vicars

1899	T. P. BROCKLEHURST
1900	William LONDON c.1862–1923
1923	Henry G. BAKER c.1862–1945
1945	Cyril R. BROWN c.1896–1990
1955	John STONEHOUSE, RC priest 1919, Anglican 1940
1962	Justice BECKE MBE c.1908–
1966	Richard LEWIS b.1935. 1990 Dean, Wells Cathedral
1972	Brian L. HAMMOND b.1931. 1980–6 Rural Dean Reigate 1983–92 Hon Canon Southwark
1988	Eric C. LAST 1930–
1997	Marian S. RANDALL

The Epiphany

1955	Jack CLARK
1959	John R. DUDLEY
1968	Hector M. GOULD
1977	Charles A. CROFTS 1969–76 Hon Canon St. Albans
1980	– none –
1989	Christine WHEELER (née Millar)
1997	Christine LATHAM

Smales saddlery, London Road South

Herbert Chopping's bakery, 27 Nutfield Road

Those in trade and transport

Jim Charman was one of those who has been in the village long enough to recall how very different it was when he was young[35], and in particular how varied the different trades and services that were carried on before the supermarket made so many of them redundant. Kelly's directory for the early part of the century lists in the High Street and Nutfield Road such occupations as baker, butcher, fruiterer, grocer and drapers, tailor, laundress, confectioner, banker, printer, blacksmith, cobbler, coal merchant, chimney sweep and cycle engineer. This was at a time when most people wore hats, could ride a horse, ate according to what was in season, had their purchases measured and wrapped (some even delivered), and paid for them in shillings and pence.

One of Merstham's oldest local trading families was the **Smale** family, saddler and harness maker, who came to Merstham from Exeter to take advantage of the London-to-Brighton coach trade in 1831. At the beginning of the twentieth century the business was still being carried out, mainly for farmers, by Mrs. Eliza Smale and her son from behind the huge wheel-shaped window of what is now called "The Old Saddlery" at the junction of the High Street and London Road South. The room next to it was the shop in which one could purchase the leather horse gear, aprons, ropes (St. Katharine's bell-ropes came from here) and horse brasses, enscribed "A. Smale, maker, Merstham". After the First World War, it was the son, Alfred and his wife Kate, who lived next door in what is now called "Old Tye Place" with their daughter, Dorothy. There were still plenty of working horses up to and including the Second World War but, when Alfred died in 1928, Kate could not travel around the county the way he had done and, although she was still listed as "harness maker" in 1938, the business declined. The buildings were sold and Dorothy moved to a house at the Eastern end of Albury Road.

As the car became the common form of transport, so high streets became awkward to visit, which gave rise to the multi-storey car parks built in the larger towns in the 1960s, attracting people from a larger catchment area than before.

---

[35] He made a recent cassette recording of his memories of Merstham in the 1920s

This certainly contributed to the reduced use of local village stores, but in the last two decades, it has been increasing commercial property rent and rates, and, of course, competition from the new purpose-built supermarkets that made village shops selling basic, low margin, commodities increasingly uneconomic. A comparison of the description[36] of the High Street area between 1938 and 1998, gives some idea of how very different village-based shops have become:

No. (now): 1938

1998

	1938	1998
	"The Feathers" Hotel (Harry Atkins)	*"The Feathers"* restaurant
40	Cobbler (Willy and Richard Smith)	Private residence
38	Butchers (Tom Joyce[37])	"D" Signmakers
34	Baptist mission chapel	Merstham Antiques
32	Confectioners ("Punch" Evans)	Party Shop
30	Bakers (Broad, t.a. Partridge's)	Gervaise Cottage
28	Mrs. Underwood's house	Vista Sports
26	Drapers (Underwoods)	The Village Bakers
24	Fruiterer and greengrocers (Harry Ball & Son)	Merstham Glass
22	Tailors (Fred Barwell)	Flint Cottage
20		John's Army Surplus
18	Grocers and fishmongers (George Uridge)	Off License (Victoria wine)
16		Violins (David & Emma Newton)
12	Lloyds Bank Ltd.	Music (David & Emma Newton)
10	Hairdressers (Hearden's)	Post Office
6	*later* Annette's Wool Store	Barnard Interiors
2	Barclays Bank Ltd.	Chartered surveyor's office (P. Miles)
1	*"Cottage of Content"* pub (Ben. Wilkinson)	Tavern House private residence

---

[36] For an idea of how much more the village has altered over the full century, see Mr. Woodhouse's account of the village in 1907, as recalled in Mary Morris' *History of Merstham* (pp 75-8)
[37] The Joyce family lived in "Hawthornden", later the home of the Francis family, now "Cherrycob House".

Few expect small traders to last more than a generation, but Portland Drive demonstrates how much shorter has become the expected "shelf life" of a precarious local shop:

No.	1958	1998
2	Grocers (C. B. Buttner)	Newsagents (Martins) & P.O.
4	Newsagents (J. Bailey)	Fish & Chips
16	Butchers (Dewhursts Ltd)	Video hire
18	Fruiterer (J. Henderson)	Merstham carpets
20	Toy shop (Matthewson)	Hardware
22	Hardware (Goodrich Ltd)	Dry cleaners (Goodrich)
36	Doric Cleaners (A. Beswick)	Plumbing and electrical (AJM)
38	Tobacconist and post office	Chinese take-away
42	Edgar's Grocers (F Meyers Ltd.)	Fruit and veg.
44	Butcher (J Henley Oscar)	Butchers (The Tender Joint)
46	Grocers (A. Alfreds)	*vacant* (ex optician)
48	Off license (St. Giles Taverns Ltd.)	Off license (Drinks Cabin)

It has been a gradual change, and the retail businesses in Nutfield Road have not changed as rapidly as those in the High Street and Portland Drive. As Bevis Hillier puts it: "Unlike Old Merstham, South Merstham hasn't changed a jot. To go there is to step back into the 1950s. The grocer, the baker, the butcher are in the same place, as is the sweet shop, then called the *Bon-Bon*, where we kids would buy the most delicious ice-lollies".

In terms of manufacturing, the adjacent Holmethorpe estate was the nearest employer. Except, that is, for a pre-Green Belt building in Nutfield Road that originally housed Howard Price Ltd., a bed manufacturer. It is now occupied by C.T.S. which makes the automatic ticket gates for the London underground.

So much of this way of life has changed that those of us born half way through the century forget that this is all within the living memory of those born before. Several generations were raised in this century, but the life expectancy of a single generation covers it all: If we take Henry **Sargant** as an example, we get an interesting picture of a local entrepreneur responding to the demands of his time: Eldest of eight children, he left school in 1899 as soon as then legally possible, at the age of 10, to help his father who was the Earlswood coal merchant. In 1905 he was taking the horse-drawn, night-time, mail wagon from the sorting office to Dorking, at an age when he could still be frightened of seeing ghosts in Buckland churchyard! But this gave him the experience to set up a haulage business in Redhill, buying "Kelly lorries" from the Army after the First World War, suitably converted to his needs by his brother, Percy. In the 1920's he and his wife, Blanche (who had the advantage of being able to read and write properly), bought land at Godstone and at the junction of Battlebridge and Nutfield Roads opposite All Saints. The origin of Charlie Rider's vehicle repairers is the Sargant's 1932 vehicle spraying works. He excavated sand at both holdings for delivery to the local building sites, right up to the Second World War. The story of how a German land mine made another pit next to Sargant's one is told elsewhere. The Canadian Army filled that one, and, at the end of the War, Henry buried his lorries in his own pit, creating a clear green opposite the Church. He and his wife had no children and, in 1948, volunteered to give this area of land as a Garden of Remembrance on condition that it never be developed. Although accepted by popular ballot, it took until 1954 for the Merstham War Memorial Committee (chaired by Col. Jock Hunter) to convince the Borough Council, since when this piece of land has served South Merstham as a useful open space, but without any plaque indicating its origin or intent. In 1988 Blanche died and Henry, who had been so close to her for so long, chose to follow her. The last of his generation, Reg, died in 1995, aged 95, bringing the average life span of these 8 children to 90 years each.

Further down Nutfield Road (no. 131) on the East side just beyond the former Methodist chapel was a Sand and Brick works, run by Ray & Sons of Coulsdon. There was quite a substantial water-filled pit in a site of about 15 acres, with a dredger pumping the soaking sand into drainage hoppers. This was the scene of a tragic accident on a hot Sunday afternoon in 1928 or 1929 when the manager took his wife and daughter out in a rowing boat. It capsized and both ladies were drowned. The company also dug out clay and made bricks on the site. Percy Brown recalls from his youth how the trade had its own language: Digging and loading the clay was "homicking"; shaping them was "pugging". The wet bricks were laid on "hacks", the drying frames, some hundred yards long; each brick had to be adjusted periodically to dry out fully and this was the "skintling" process; groups of bricks were then "crowded" in high-boarded barrows to be taken to be fired in the kiln. The South Merstham Sand and Brick Company, as it became, was bought by Wates the builders and it was this company that filled in the site and developed Wycliffe Gardens in 1964. This small estate was intended as starter homes for young executives, so that, once the residents were embroiled in legal wrangling with Wates over compensation for the subsequent subsidence, it was not surprising that one of them, Mark Doswell, was a lawyer, which proved very useful to his fellow residents. He has since moved on to international law, based near Zurich.

When the Jolliffe family acquired the Merstham estate in 1788, one of the priorities was to establish an alternative London toll road to the one built via Reigate. When they achieved this, and the early horse-powered railway, in the early 19th Century, they established the main London to Brighton route that was to be used initially by coach and horse and then by every subsequent form of transport. At the beginning of the 20th Century, the road that was later called the A23 was a favourite cycling route, the corner by *The Feathers* being known as "Gossip Corner" where the young of the day could indulge in the age-old pastimes of showing off and studying form. It was "a famous Sunday morning meeting place for cyclists down South and one that has retained its popularity for years"[38]. Geoffrey Lloyd ran a cycle repair shop on the Western side of the High Street next to William Friend & Son, the blacksmiths, but neither business survived the Second World War, after which cycling became mainly a children's occupation. Since the 1980s, however, Merstham has been invaded each June by the annual London-to-Brighton cycle run, the High Street only being available for this as a result of most through traffic using the alternative M23. The omnibus was the next popular form of transport: Merstham was connected to Redhill and Reigate by the East Surrey Traction Co. Ltd. in 1911 and, less popular, to London in 1913 by the London General Omnibus Co. Ltd., which was also responsible for disgorging hundreds of London trippers into what was then the furthest foray into the country by the metropolitan bus companies. Although the first Veteran Car run down the road was in 1896, it was another 30 years before it became an annual event. Motor cars were a rarity until the 1930s and not a real nuisance to the community until after the end of petrol rationing in May 1950. The steady increase in car ownership then completed the present picture of the village. Initially the only garage was Willoughby's (later Hardy & Baldry) on a part of London Road North that went with the M25 bridge. Post war, it had a rival, Valley View garage (later

---

[38] Extract from an article in the *Cycling* journal of 1895, quoted in the Country Post, August 1971.

Shackletons) in Station Road. The imposing modern "Q8"[39] garage forecourt was the site of the local vet's practice, so completely has the tyre replaced the hoof.

It was the railways, though, that gave Merstham its main raison d'être this century (and its early involvement in the first pre-steam public railways is reflected in two of its local pub names). The present station is a very sad reflection of what was for so long the lifeblood of the community that lived here. The station buildings had been substantially redeveloped in 1905, when the current footbridge was erected. At that time, there was a station-master with authority over half a dozen shift staff, including porters for the goods traffic and the signalmen who ran the classic LBSC signal box around the clock. This building was demolished in the 1980s, as was the period canopy on the East side to accommodate the raised rail for trains that were to go straight through without stopping. Steam engines were replaced by electrically-powered ones in 1932, making the surrounding area considerably cleaner. Although gas was the standard form of station lighting long after private residences had switched to electricity, the visiting Canadians made Merstham station the first on this line to be lighted, subject to the black-out restrictions, by electricity in 1940. At the same time sidings were built between the two through lines. At the end was a large water hole, fed by the remnant of the mill stream. Before the war this had been an unofficial swimming pool to the local lads. One might guess that it was the same grown up lads who told tales of it containing an old sunken steam engine complete with brass lamps etc. When the railway bridges had to be built for the new motorway, it took a couple of weeks arguing to convince the railway authorities, collectors and television, that it did not exist. Or does it? Of the many station-masters of Merstham, probably John Harman is best remembered, the last to live in the house that used to stand where the station car park now lies. The next generation of commuters still recalls Brian Pyke, the manager for a couple of decades, with affection. Surprisingly, he never lived in the village, but commuted daily from Horley. Then there was a typical W. H. Smith & Son stall in the building, run by Norman Worsfold in the 1980s. Sadly an arsonist burnt out his stall shortly after he bought the business and, despite offers of support from every part of Merstham, he understandably left

---

[39] Kuwaiti Petroleum Company.

the village altogether. It was a time when there was a spate (short-lived, luckily) of glue-sniffing and vandalism; another act of arson destroyed the village cricket pavilion, but at least that was replaced and, indeed, is more practical and larger.

Of the many people associated with the railway, the main one locally was Frank **Prior**. He was trained as a chartered civil engineer with the Great Western Railway, having to change careers, like so many of that generation, in the Great Depression. So he joined the army and was commissioned into the Royal Engineers in 1935. On the outbreak of war in '39, he raised and accompanied a railway construction company for that short-lived expedition to France. After a spell dealing with bomb damage in the London area, Col. Frank Prior was posted to the Far East, where he was responsible for the transport troops supporting the 14th Army in Burma, for which he got his OBE. He returned to civilian life after the war and, in 1952, came to Merstham with his new role as Divisional Engineer for London East region of the recently nationalised British Rail, Southern Region. This meant he was responsible for about 2,000 staff, all the structures and tracks of the Southern Railway in London (except Waterloo) and an area in a radius of about 25-30 miles from there. He and his wife, Rosemary, raised their two sons at Hazelton on Battlebridge Lane, Rosemary being active in the Mothers Union, Women's Institute and on the board of local schools. In 1965 they moved to London Road North, Hazelton being pulled down (its timbers were in poor condition) and blocks of maisonettes erected in its place. All Saints' loss was St. Katharine's gain, though the Priors kept in touch with friends from both parishes. By the time Frank retired in 1971 he was responsible for the maintenance of the whole of Southern Region. When their "Baldwyns" house and garden became too large to manage, they moved into a flat in The Grange. Although Rosemary died in 1995, Frank is likely to see in the next millenium. Included in his guests for his 90th birthday party in July 1998 held in Rookwood Hotel, were the Stephens, Anthony returning once again to the house in which he was raised, and only months before it became a Chinese restaurant. Change is constant in Merstham, and it would be a dull place if it were not so.

Postscript

At the beginning of this century "Merstham" was a postal area in its own right, covering areas of neighbouring parishes (some of those in Chaldon's Hill Top Lane area, Gatton, and Warwick Wold, were part of Merstham for postal purposes). At that time Merstham had its own Telephone Exchange (the front room of a house on the West side of the High Street) and Postal Sorting Office, later amalgamated in a new, purpose-built building between the Village Hall and the car dealers in Station Road. The staff were in a smart uniform best remembered for their pill-box hats, and were equipped with, at best, a bicycle. In 1919 a 24 year old postman, Bill **Cox**, was transferred to Merstham, after having seen active service, and been wounded, in Flanders. He was typically a founding member of the Village Club and the Merstham branch of the British Legion. By the late '20s his job was mechanised and he received a motor bike and sidecar which made the journey up Shepherd's Hill, for example, a lot easier. In due course he was equipped with the standard post office red delivery van. He and his family lived in Endsleigh Road, a convenient location, as it turned out, from which to help deal with the after-effects of the land-mine explosion. For the blast shook the soot out of every nearby chimney and it turned out the Cox home was the only one to be able to provide a hot bath for their many neighbours to remove the grime from their bodies the following morning! In the early '50s, Merstham's sorting office operation was transferred to Redhill and the automated exchanges were similarly concentrated elsewhere. Bill Cox retired in 1955 with the Imperial Service medal to add to his Queen's Coronation medal. On the face of it, no more than one would expect for a dedicated employee. What made Bill Cox very special to Merstham, however, was the depth of kindness he showed to all his customers. During the second war, he was acutely aware of the importance of news from the front and handled his messenger role with great care and tact. Even his wife was unaware of some of the extra efforts he made, such as making an unscheduled delivery so that an anxious mother would not have to wait until after the weekend for news of her son. Among the tokens he received on his retirement was a scroll, 3ft by 2ft, which contained the signature of nearly every resident of his rounds. This is what Merstham was all about in this recent century.

Index

Adams, Michael, 39
Agate, Charles, 29
Albury Road, 6, 8, 17, 33, 34, 37, 39, 43, 47, 51, 75, 79, 86, 95
Aldridge, Miss Alice, 26
Alleyn, Tim, 11, 22, 55, 61, 70, 71, 89
Atkins, Harry, 96
Augarde, Mrs F., 17, 79, 80
Anderson, Sir John, 2, 49, 58–60
Anderson, Mrs. Joy, 35, 36
Auton, Miss, 69
Ayres, Rev. Ronald, 87, 93
Baker, Rev. Henry, 86, 87, 93
Ball, Arthur, 71
Ball, Charles, 26
Ball, Harry, 96
Barratt, Albert, 37, 39
Batchelor, Laura, 37, 73
Bateman, Mrs., 42
Battersby, Bob, 61
Battiscombe Miss, 28
Battlebridge Lane, 6, 34, 40, 62, 74, 98, 101
Becke, Rev. Justice, 89–90, 93
Beech Road, 42, 70, 71, 80
Bennett, P. M., 63
Benson, Lord, 23
Benson, Laurie, 89
Biddell, Rev. John, 93
Biggs, Ronald, 72–73
Birt, Kenny, 47
Bletchingley Road, 10, 26, 29, 41, 54, 55, 56, 63, 80, 89
Bolsover Grove, 10, 70, 71
Bourne Road, 37, 87
Bowring, Cyril, 21, 36
Bristow, E., 52
British Legion, 2, 9, 27, 44, 46–47, 48, 79, 103
Brook Road, 8, 35, 51, 86
Brown, Rev. Cyril, 87, 89, 93
Brown, Percy, 5, 6, 98
Bull family, 27, 28, 56, 57
Bush, Stuart, 53
Bushetts Grove, 34, 70
Callow family, 5, 22, 36, 37
Campbell, A. Doon, 74

Campbell, Sybil, 70
Campbell, Sir Walter and Lady, 47, 59
Carden, Bruce, 70
Charman, Jim, 5, 95
Chapman, William, 55
Charlesworth Sgt., 36
Chart, Frank and Dennis, 37
Chatterton, Rt Rev. Eyre, 93
Chesterton Drive, 39
Church Hill, 7, 16, 24, 36, 47, 50, 54, 58, 70, 75, 76, 80, 81, 84
Clark, Rev. Jack, 87, 93
Clark, Mary, 86
Clarke, Mrs. Muriel, 40, 55, 56
Cole, Dr. Gwen, 81
Colebrooke, 11, 53
Colman, Sir Jeremiah, 6, 8, 33, 62, 63, 65, 85
Connaught, Princess Arthur of, 68–69
Constant, Roger, 24, 40
Copper, C., 36
Cox, Bill, 29, 103
Cox, Doris, 29
Craker, Mr., 63
Crickett, Dr. Henry, 78
Crofts, Rev. Charles, 93
Crosfield, Joyce, 5, 24, 70, 71
Crossways, The, 24, 55
Danckwerts, Jim, 28, 70, 71
Davison, Sir Arthur, 42
Dawes family, 5, 45, 81
Dean's Road, 6, 45, 80
Delabole Road, 10, 29
Deverill, Jack, 7
Devon Road, 33, 54, 62, 74, 86, 90
Donovan, A., 55
Doswell, Mark, 99
Downs family, 65
Doyle, Paddy, 89
Dudley, Rev. John, 89, 93
Dulwich (Alleyns) College, 32, 90
Duval, Rev. Philip, 36, 40, 93
Evans, Punch, 96
Floodgate, Rev. Dennis, 93
Flower, Fr. Hugh, 93
Fogg Alan, 24

Francis family, 8–9, 54, 96
Gatton Bottom, 16, 37, 55, 70, 71, 73, 85
Gibson, Mr., 29
Gill, Miss, 29
Glassup H, 84
Gloster-Smith, Daphne, 90, 92
Goad, Col. John, 69
Goldsbrough, Carole, 5
Gould, Rev. Hector, 93
Green, Col., 49–50
Grieve family, 15–16, 27
Grosvenor, Rev. Royston, 93
Gruhn, Nora, 42
Hale, Jim, 89
Hamlin, Peter and Ruth, 42
Hammond, Rev. Brian, 93
Hammond, Dr. John, 81–82
Hancock, Mr., 63
Harman, John, 100
Harris, George, 69
Harrison M., 46, 52
Harps Oak Lane, 16, 22, 24, 43, 52, 69, 70, 72, 73
Hawthorns School, 15, 17, 27, 28, 57, 69, 81
Hazel, Newton, 33–34, 44, 54
Heslop, R.N., 55
Hicks, Sir Seymour, 30, 32
Hill, Fr. Michael, 93
Hill, Richard, 40
Hillier, Jack and Bevis, 75–76, 97
Hills, Dr. Tom, 81
Hilton-Sergeant, Gen. F., 52
Hitchins, Phil, 55
Hoffer, Mr., 26
Hope Mason, Miss., 28
Hopper, Rev. John, 93
Houlder, Howard, 87
Hughes, Jack and Mary, 92
Hummel, Miss. Cecile, 27–28, 35, 37
Hunt, G., 54
Hunter, Col. Jock, 22–23, 24, 40, 55, 98
Hylton, Lord, 6, 7, 8, 10, 16, 30, 39, 41, 43, 52, 64, 84
Jarmen, Miss, 29
Jarchow family, 11, 17, 30, 44, 45, 65, 67, 69, 79
Jenkins, David, 70

Johnson, Eileen, 31, 55
Joiner, J, 63
Jolliffe family – see Hylton
Joyce, Tom, 34, 96
Kennedy, Denise, 35, 37
Kee, Daniel, 56
Kirk, Geoffrey, 70–71
Lachelin, family, 23–24, 57
Lally, Gwen, 69
Lambert, Sir David, 49, 81
Last, Rev. Eric, 93
Laxton Gardens, 70
Leader, Bob, 70, 71
Lee, John, 22
Leonard, Sir John and Lady, 70, 72
Lewis, Rev. Richard, 90, 93
Lewis, Linda, 41
Lilley, Fred, 54, 55
Lloyd, Geoffrey, 99
London, Rev. W., 85, 93
London Rd. North, 19, 41, 43, 54, 56, 61, 82, 99, 101
London Rd. South, 7, 12, 17, 44, 45, 54, 55, 62, 69, 78, 95
Longley, Ken, 89
Longshaw, Les, 90
Maiklem family, 52–53
Malmestone Av., 55, 63, 89
Marshall, Maj., 47
Matthewman family, 39, 46
McCarthy, Jack, 89
Melton Road, 6, 7
Merstham Aid Project, 56, 92
Merstham Amateur Dramatics Soc. 3, 11, 27, 30, 35–37, 55, 58, 67, 69, 75
Merstham Boy Scouts, 2, 19, 33, 50, 84
Merstham Cricket Club, 9, 19, 20, 21, 22, 27, 32, 64, 67, 78, 81, 101
Merstham Football Club, 32–33, 47
Merstham Horticultural Society, 2, 6, 9, 19, 22, 63
Merstham Nursing Association, 17, 44, 65
Merstham Peace Committee, 22, 37, 80, 92
Merstham Primary School, 7, 17, 26–27, 29, 45

Merstham Protection Society, 22, 58
Merstham Rifle Club, 18
Merstham Society, The, 3, 9, 22, 27–28, 42, 52, 55, 61, 71, 72, 75, 77
Merstham Village Club, 18, 21, 32, 46–47, 67, 103
Merstham Village Hall, 3, 19, 21, 31, 36, 37, 39, 40, 42, 46–47, 87, 103
Merstham Women's Institute, 2, 3, 7, 19, 24, 36, 37, 40–41, 67, 77, 79, 81, 85, 101
Merstham Youth Club, 9, 36, 39–40, 56, 65, 87
Millar, Christine, 90, 93
Mold, John, 55
Monger, Albert, 55, 71
Monson, Lord, 6
Moore, Alan, 24
Moore, Muriel, 55
Morris family, 5, 50, 52, 96
Mountford, Ron, 12
Moy, Arthur, 22
Netherne Hospital, 54, 81, 92
Newsome, Barry, 40, 55, 56
Newton, David, 42, 96
Nicol, R. S., 6–7, 63
Nicholson, H. and family, 18, 22
Nicholson, W., 16,
Nightingale H. "Punch", 27
Nokvam, Dr. Otto, 83
Nutfield Road, 4, 6–9, 45, 54, 55, 63, 79, 83, 86, 87, 95–98
O'Driscoll, Pat, 71
Oelman, Sydney, 55
Ogilvie, Ian, 12
Oliver, Jim, 5, 41
Oram family, 9–10
Orange, Gladys, 80
Passmore, Alfred, 5
Pearch, Jean, 70, 71
Pelly, family, 17, 63, 64–65
Perkins, Bill, 6, 9
Peters family, 10, 45–46
Philanthropic Soc., Royal, 24
Pink, J and S. T., 9–10, 19, 54
Poole, Dame Anne, 58
Poole, Rev. Joseph, 28, 67, 89, 93
Portland Drive, 10, 41, 73, 97

Pratt, Mr., 29
Prentice, Ron, 21–22
Preston, I. K., 77
Prevett, Fred, 34, 38
Priddy, Harriet, 26
Prior, Col. Frank, 101
Prior, Stephen, 73
Puckle, H. Leonard, 16, 19
Pullinger, J. E. and Carette, 70, 72
Pyke, Brian, 100
Quality Street, 3, 7, 8, 11, 13, 18, 22, 26, 28, 30, 32, 34, 36, 47, 50, 52, 58, 60, 65, 67, 70, 77, 79, 84, 91
Quihampton, John, 54
Radstock Way, 10, 39, 55, 56, 64, 70
Randall, Marian, 90, 93
Redd, Dr. Roger, 80,
Rider, Charlie, 98
Robinson. Rev. A., 93
Rockshaw Road, 2, 7, 18, 21–24, 34, 47, 49, 52, 55–58, 61, 63, 70–72, 75, 77, 78, 80, 85
Roffey, family, 17, 27, 44, 65, 67
Rogers, Rev. A., 85
Rohmer, Sax, 74
Rolls, Col. Norman, 47
Ryder, Paul, 70
Sargant, Henry, 97–98
Seager, Stephen, 55
Searle, George, 54, 55–56, 70,71
Sellon, Percy, 18, 54
School Hill, 26, 42, 45, 46, 70, 71, 81
Shaw, Ron, 34, 45, 86
Sheehan, Nurse, 80
Sheehy, Fr. Thomas, 89, 93
Shepherds Hill, 42, 45, 50, 52, 69, 70, 71, 77, 103
Shott, R., 54
Simpson, Mark, 55
Smale family, 95
Smalley, Peter, 56
Smith, Rev. John, 93
Smith, Willy, 32, 96
Smythies, B., 76
Stacey, Harrie and family, 7, 43, 70
Stanway, Drs., 77
Stephens family, 5, 7, 8, 16–18, 27, 28, 33, 37, 44, 45, 58, 65, 81, 101

Stewart, Miss A., 47
Stonehouse, Rev. John, 31, 89, 93
Stradling, Maurice, 15, 43, 52, 64
Stribbling, family, 8, 29, 43
Sunstone Grove, 29
Sutton Gardens, 92
Tayler, Dr. Robert, 37, 62, 80
Taynton Drive, 29, 53, 63, 70, 89
Terriss, Ellaline – see Hicks
Thompson, Mr., 34
Thurston Mrs., 42
Toms family, 38, 39, 75
Topham Richardson family, 16, 19, 70, 79
Trigg, Dr., 80
Tucker, Dr. John, 79–81
Uridge, George, 96
Underwoods, 96
Walker family, 16, 18
Wall, Charles, 26–27, 39
Warren, Miss, 29
Warwick Wold, 41, 64, 70, 77, 80, 103
Watney family, 19, 57
Watson, Paxton and Georgina, 7, 8, 45, 47, 65, 79
Watts – see Sheehan
Webbe, family, 12, 17, 22, 36, 57–58
Webber, Edward, 58
Webber, Dr. Leonard, 81
Weir, family, 47, 54, 62, 69, 70, 78–79
Weldon Way, 33, 40, 47, 55, 87
Wells, family, 19, 45, 62–63, 86
West, John, 45
Wheeler, Christine – see Millar
Wheeler, Sir Charles, 76–77
Whitaker, family, 8, 9, 69, 70
White, Sir Dick, 11, 59, 60–61
White, Peter, 77
Wicks, Ted, 42
Wilkinson, Rev. A. E., 85–86, 93
Wilkinson, Ben, 96
Williamson, Skip, 38, 39–40, 87
Wolfendale, Rev. George, 86–87
Woodhouse, family, 33, 50, 84–85, 93
Woodman, Fr. Bennett, 93
Worsfold, Norman, 5, 15, 29, 100
Wycliffe Gardens, 98

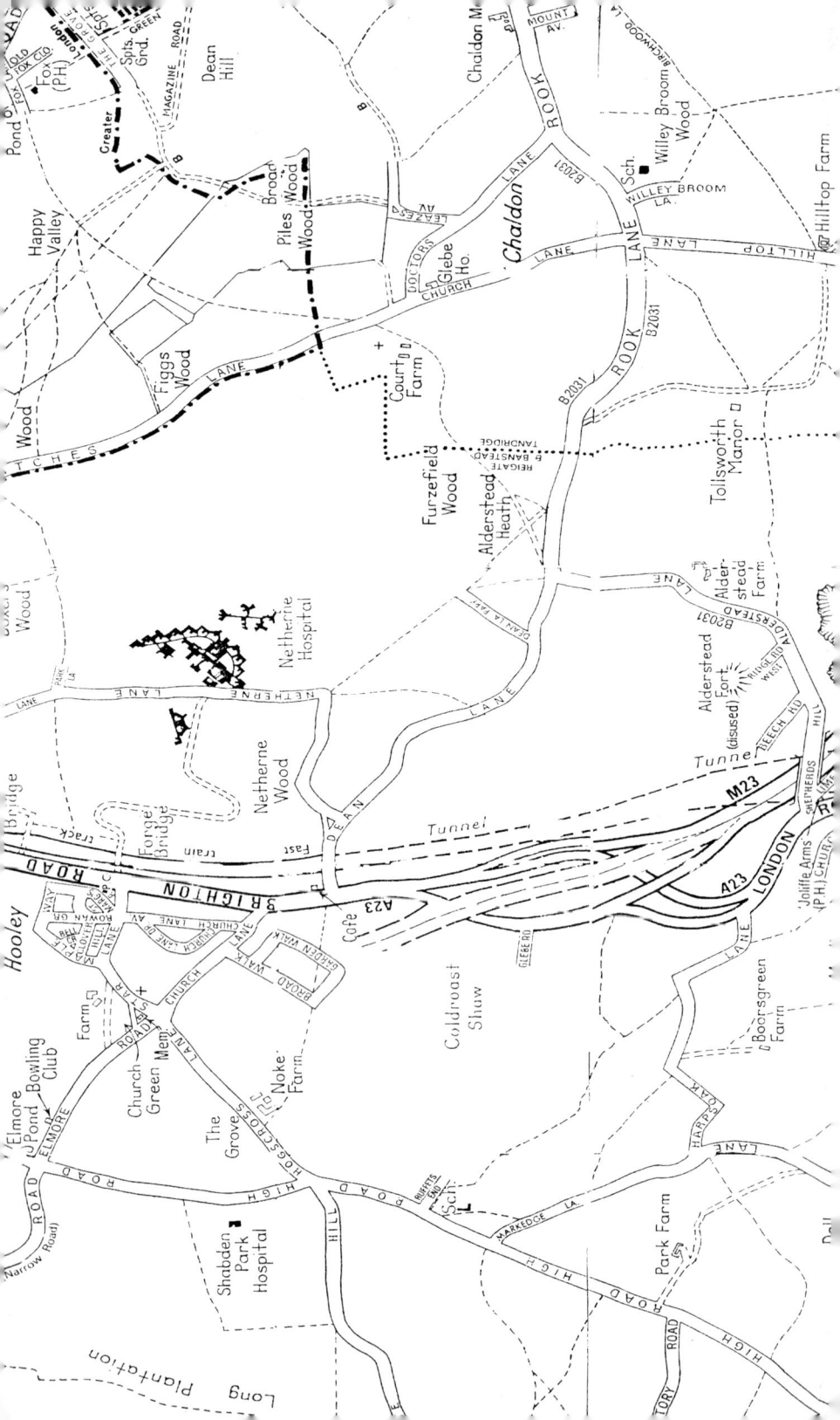